WUNDERKEYS®
PRIMER PIANO BOOK ONE

PRIMER
BOOK ONE

WunderKeys Primer Piano Book One by Andrea and Trevor Dow
Copyright © 2017 Teach Music Today Learning Solutions
www.teachpianotoday.com and www.wunderkeys.com

All Rights Reserved. This book or parts thereof may not be reproduced in any form, stored in any retrieval system, or transmitted in any form by any means - electronic, mechanical, photocopy, recording, or otherwise - without prior written permission of the publisher, except as provided by copyright law.

WunderKeys® is a registered trademark of Andrea and Trevor Dow (Teach Music Today Learning Solutions) in the U.S.A. and Canada

An Introduction To WunderKeys

When I left home for college many years ago, I took with me a trunkful of clothes, a few pairs of shoes, a blanket, a pillow, and my favorite book, *Harold and the Purple Crayon*.

The book was torn, tattered, and loved to death.

As a young child, I needed my parents' help to cross the street or tie my shoes, but when I flipped through the pages of *Harold and the Purple Crayon*, I entered a world of inspiring adventures where I could do anything and be anyone.

So when I created WunderKeys with my husband, Trevor, we did so with one overriding goal in mind: to produce **piano method books** that would one day be packed into the trunk of a car – torn, tattered, and loved to death by a lifelong music student starting out on a new adventure.

Thank you for taking your piano students on our "wunderful" journey through music.

Andrea and Trevor Dow

Primer 1

Jam-packed with age-appropriate piano pieces, off-the-bench activities, and game-based learning, WunderKeys Primer Piano Book 1 reinforces keyboard awareness and early note reading in an environment carefully crafted to meet the physical capabilities of young piano students. The book's engaging illustrations, hilarious dialogue, and step-by-step scaffolding approach combine to create the resource that piano teachers, piano parents, and piano students have been waiting for. In WunderKeys Primer Piano Book 1, students will:

1. Gain an understanding of the keyboard
2. Read rhythmic notation and develop aural awareness
3. Explore correct piano posture and hand shape
4. Learn the musical alphabet
5. Identify notes on treble and bass staves
6. Play pieces accessible to small hands
7. Explore dynamics and time signatures

Note: The story-based instructions in this book are intended to be read aloud.

A Grand Adventure

Maxine, your new piano comes today. Aren't you excited?

I'm nervous that Gary will drop it down the stairs.

As long as that grizzly doesn't smell any honey, everything will be fine. Would you like to join us as we learn to play the piano?

Finger Number Fun

To help us play the piano, our fingers are given numbers. I will say a finger number. Wiggle your matching right-hand (RH) and left-hand (LH) fingers.

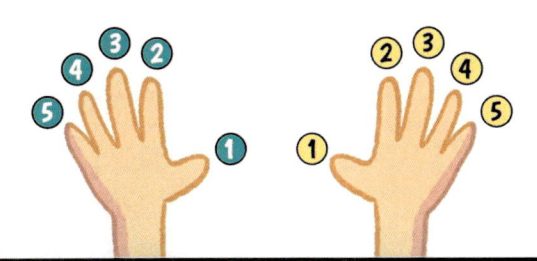

1. On a piece of paper I will draw a squiggly line that begins at the top and ends at the bottom. I will place five coins at the top of the paper.

2. Roll a die. Using your **RH finger that matches** the number rolled, slide a coin along the line from the start to the finish (roll again if a "6" is displayed). Keep rolling until all five coins have been moved along the line.

3. Let's play again using your LH fingers.

A Grand Adventure

Let's Calm Maxine With Music

Oh no! Gary will smell the honeysuckles by my door!

Hold up your RH 2 finger. Play sounds on white keys. Play sounds on black keys.

On the piano, **black keys** are arranged in groups of two and groups of three. Using your RH 2 and 3 fingers, play every group of two black keys, moving from low to high. Using your LH 3 and 2 fingers, play every group of two black keys, moving from high to low.

Oh... and there is a honeydew in my garden. Gary is going to drop my piano for sure.

I think Gary's after a different kind of honey. Now, are you ready to learn more?

Let's Help Maxine Find Groups Of Three

Use your LH 4, 3, and 2 fingers to press down a group of **three black keys**. Play every group of three black keys on the keyboard, moving from low to high then high to low.

Use your RH 2, 3, and 4 fingers to press down a group of three black keys. Play every group of three black keys on the keyboard, moving from low to high then high to low.

That was fun, but I need to get to Gary. Bye!

A Grand Adventure

Tap the numbers in the practice pieces below using your matching fingers.

Listen to me play each practice piece on groups of black keys.

Now it's your turn to play. Are you using the correct fingers? Hands?

Practice On The Pathway

Right Hand — RH   2   2   3   3

Left Hand — LH   3   2   3   2

Right Hand — RH   3   3   4   5

Left Hand — LH   2   3   3   4

A Grand Adventure

1. Let me demonstrate what "good" piano posture looks like. Let me demonstrate what "poor" piano posture looks like.

2. Can you show me "good" piano posture? "Poor" piano posture? Play the pieces below using "good" piano posture.

Paw Power
Place your **RH 2 and 3** on a group of two black keys.

RH: 2 2 3 3 2 2 3 3 2 2 3 3 2 2 2 2

Huff And Puff
Place your **LH 2 and 1** on a group of two black keys.

LH: 1 1 2 2 1 2 1 2 1 1 2 2 1 2 1 2

Move And Groove
Place your **RH 2, 3, and 4** on a group of three black keys.

RH: 2 3 4 3 2 3 4 3 2 3 4 3 2 2 2 2

Push And Pull
Place your **LH 5, 4, and 3** on a group of three black keys.

LH: 3 4 5 4 3 4 5 4 3 3 4 4 5 5 5 5

The dashed lines in the student part assist with visualizing directional movement and do not represent a staff.

See reverse for Game Instructions

A Grand Adventure

A Grand Adventure

Game Instructions

Note: The playing cards for *A Grand Adventure* are found at the end of this book.

Players: 2 players

Materials: one laminated game board, one button, two dice, 10 playing cards

Game Objectives:

Musical Objective: To reinforce knowledge of finger numbers
Game Objective: To land the button on the green circle or the yellow circle

Setting It Up:

Players should sit beside one another with the deck of cards placed between. Each player should have a die. The button should be placed over the red circle on the game board.

How To Play:

1. During the game, the teacher attempts to move the button toward the circle marked with the yellow dot, and the student attempts to move the button toward the circle marked with the green dot.

2. To begin, one player removes the top card from the deck and flips it over to reveal an image of a marked finger.

3. At this point, the game becomes a race. Step 4 below (while explained for Player 1 only) will be performed simultaneously by both players.

4. As soon as the card in Step 2 is revealed, Player 1 determines the finger number of the marked finger and then attempts to roll the corresponding number on her die.

5. The first player to roll the correct number on her die wins the round. If the winner is the student, the button is moved one space (one circle on the staircase) toward the circle with the green dot. If the winner is the teacher, the button is moved one space toward the circle with the yellow dot

6. Players repeat Steps 2 to 5 until the button lands on the yellow dot (the student loses the game) or the green dot (the student wins the game).

7. If all cards have been removed from the deck and the button has not landed on a circle marked with a yellow or green dot, players analyze the location of the button on the game board. If it is closer to the circle with the yellow dot, the teacher wins. If it is closer to the circle with the green dot, the student wins.

Cubs In Subs

"Gary, why are you wearing a mask and snorkel?"

"I entered my honey cakes in a contest and won a submarine!"

"A submarine? Wow! Your honey cakes must be FIN-tastic! Before you set sail, join us as we learn about note values."

Let's Show Gary How To Play Quarter Notes

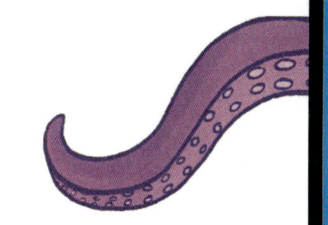

We play a sound for **one beat** when we see a quarter note. Tap each note below. Say, "sub" each time you tap. Try again, saying, "one" with each tap. Place your RH 2 and 3 on a group of two black keys. Play the quarter notes below. Each note has a number that tells you which RH finger to use.

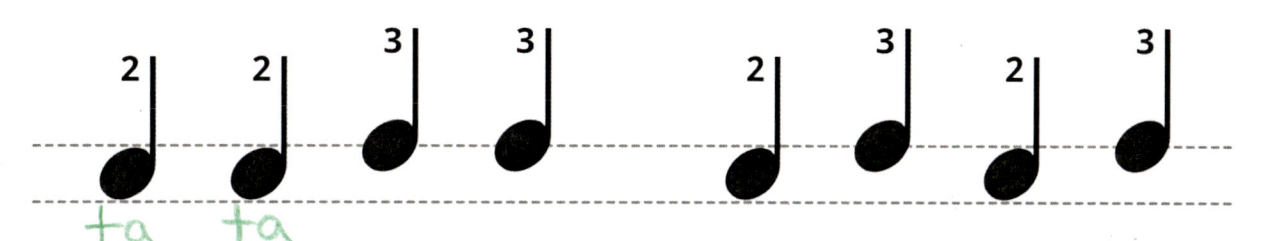

ta   ta

Cubs In Subs

Let's Show Gary How To Play Half Notes

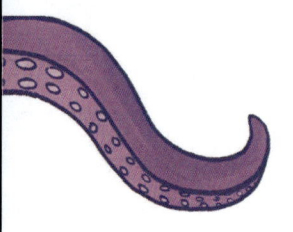

We play a sound for **two beats** when we see a half note. Tap each note below. Say, "div-ing" each time you tap. Try again, saying, "one-two" with each tap. Place your RH 1 and 2 on a group of two black keys. Play the half notes below. Count, "one-two" as you play each half note.

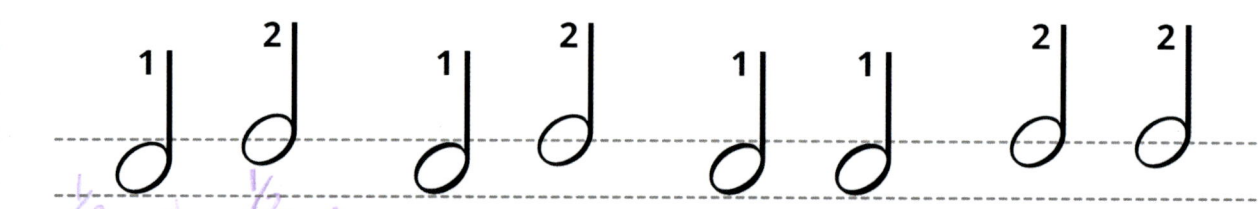

½ note   ½ note

Wait! Gary, you don't need to put flippers on yet.

I only have a few minutes! My sub is waiting and so are my friends!

Gary, please turn right-side up. We have one more thing to learn before you cast off.

Gotta run. I'll call you from my shell-phone.

RH

LH

In your music, notes with stems **pointing up** are played with the right hand, and notes with stems pointing down are played with the left hand. Let's play a game.

I will give you a coin. While I look away, place the coin in your left fist or right fist. Next, I will draw a large quarter note on a piece of paper and then turn it so its stem is pointing up or down. Look at the note and then open the hand that should play the note you see. If the coin is in your opened hand, I win the round. If not, you win the round. **Let's play four more times.**

Cubs In Subs

Listen as I clap the rhythms of the practice pieces below. Clap the rhythms back to me.

Tap each note. Say, "one" when tapping quarter notes and "one-two" when tapping half notes.

Play each practice piece. Look at the note stems. Are you using the correct hand?

Practice On The Pathway

Right Hand: 1 1 1 1 2 2   *ta   ½ note*

Right Hand: 2 3 4 3 3

Left Hand: 5 5 4 4

Left Hand: 4 4 3 2 3 4

Cubs In Subs

1. Place your hands over your knees. Now move your hands to the keys while keeping that rounded shape.

2. Look! Your fingers are curved and relaxed. Can you keep them curved while you play?

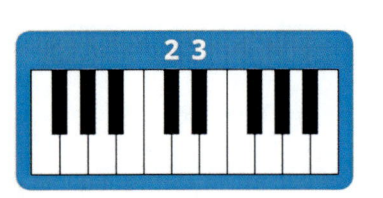

Deep Blue Sea

Clap and count the rhythm of the piece below. Place your RH 2 and 3 on a group of two black keys to play the piece. Stop at the **double bar line**.

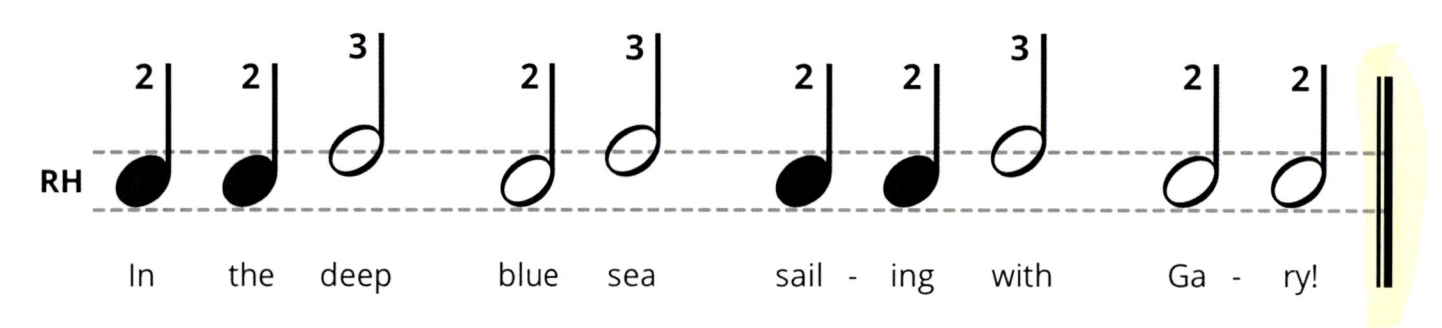

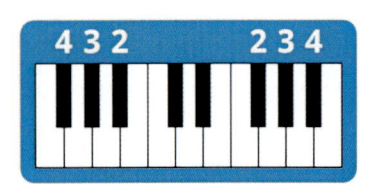

In the deep blue sea sail - ing with Ga - ry!

Submarine Song

Place your LH 4, 3, and 2 and your RH 2, 3, and 4 on groups of three black keys. Play line one and then line two. Stop at the double bar line.

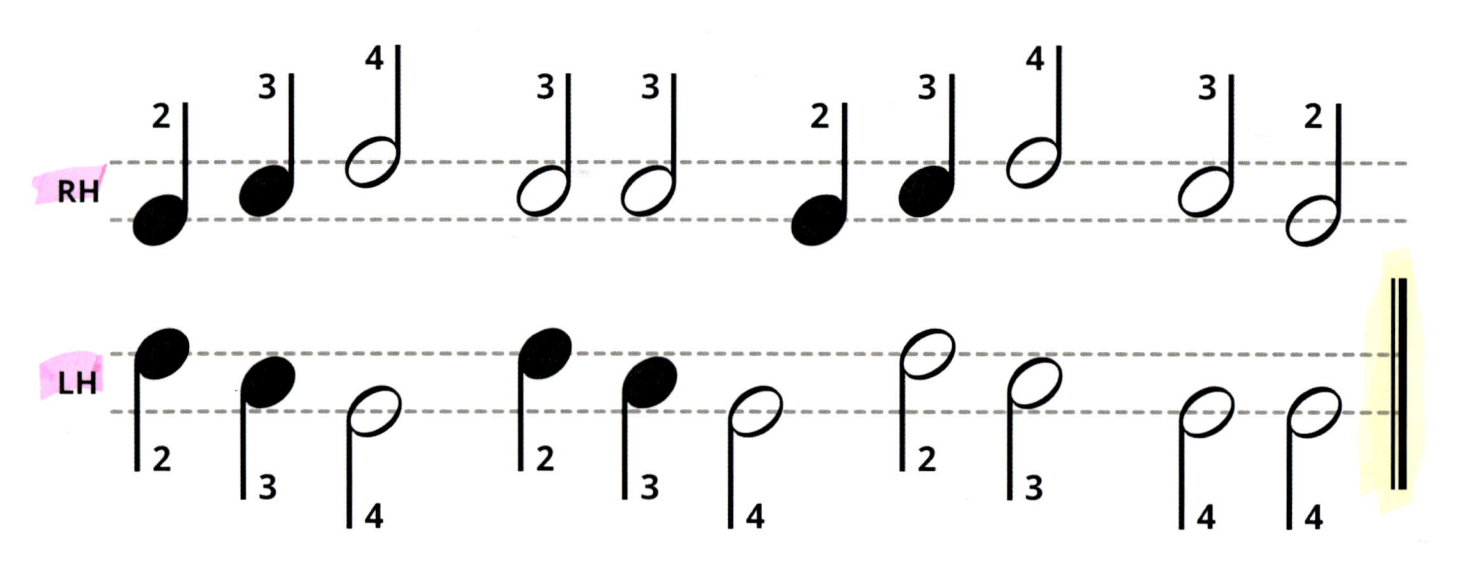

The dashed lines in the student part assist with visualizing directional movement and do not represent a staff.

Aching For Acorns

"Hello, Sheldon. You seem a little... preoccupied. What's in your mouth?"

"Mmmmpgh mmmmmmpgh mmmmpgh."

"Sheldon, you can't play the piano with acorns in your cheeks. You know the rule: no nuts in the studio! Now join us as we learn about the musical alphabet!"

The Musical Alphabet

"I already know my ABCs."

"This is a bit different, Sheldon."

1. Sheldon knows his ABCs . . . and so do you! The musical alphabet is made up of **seven letters**: A, B, C, D, E, F, and G.

2. Each white key on the piano is named after a letter from the musical alphabet.

3. Using your RH 2, play every white key, saying its letter name as you move up the keyboard.

Aching For Acorns

Oh! I hear acorns falling. I should go.

Sheldon, you can't go yet!

Let's Show Sheldon C, D, And E

The first white keys we will use to make music are **C, D, and E**. On the keyboard, find a group of two black keys. The three white keys touching the group of two black keys are C, D, and E. Use your RH 1, 2, and 3 to play all of the C, D, and Es on the keyboard.

Do you think acorn pancakes would be better than acorn waffles?

Sheldon, are you listening?

Breakfast can wait. We are going to play a game with C, D, and E and then you can... go nuts.

Let's Play Acorn Chase

Acorns are calling. Bye!

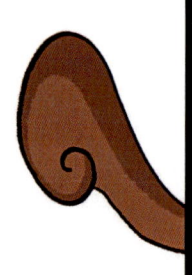

1. On the piano, I will place a game marker on Middle C. Roll a die. Move the game marker up the keyboard to the **closest key** that matches the number rolled (1 = C, 2 = D, 3 = E, 4/5 = roll again, 6 = turn is over).

2. Now I will repeat Step 1. However, instead of moving the game marker up the keyboard, I will move the game marker **down** the keyboard.

3. If the game marker is closer to the top of the keyboard after we have each had five turns, you win the game. Let's play again!

Aching For Acorns

Tap the notes below. Say, "one" when tapping quarter notes and "one-two" when tapping half notes.

I will clap the rhythms below. Can you clap the rhythms back to me?

Place your RH 1, 2, and 3 on C, D, and E. I will point to a note. Play its matching key.

Practice On The Pathway

I will point to the **treble clefs** on this page. When you see a treble clef in your music, play with your right hand.

Each piece on this page is written on a **Wunder Staff**. A Wunder Staff helps you to see if music notes are moving up, moving down, or repeating.

Place your RH 1, 2, and 3 on C, D, and E. Say the note names as you play each line of music.

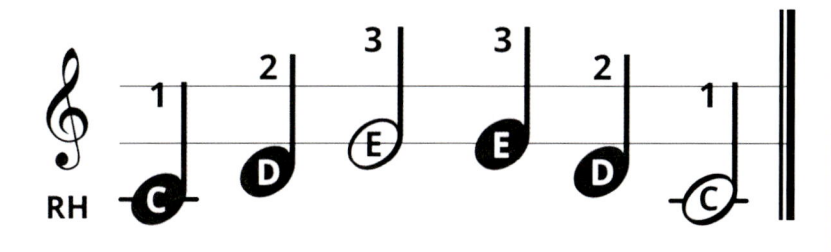

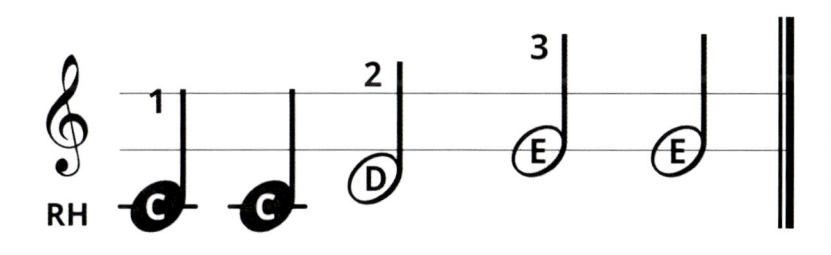

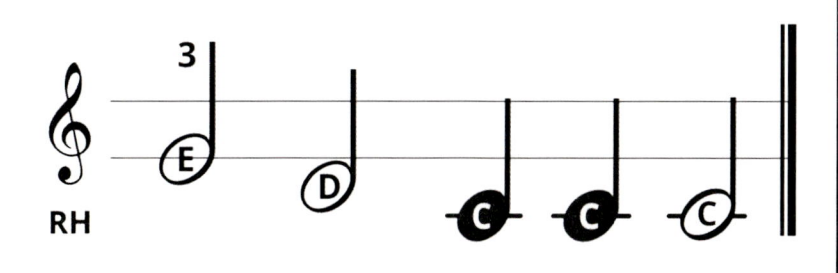

Aching For Acorns

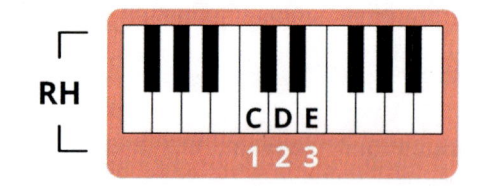

I can't... stop... eating... acorns.

RH | C D E | 1 2 3

Technique Tip: Place your curved hands on the flat surface of the piano lid. Using your fingertips and the sides of your thumbs, tap the sounds of dropping acorns. Remember this feeling when playing the music on the **Wunder Staves** below.

Shake The Tree

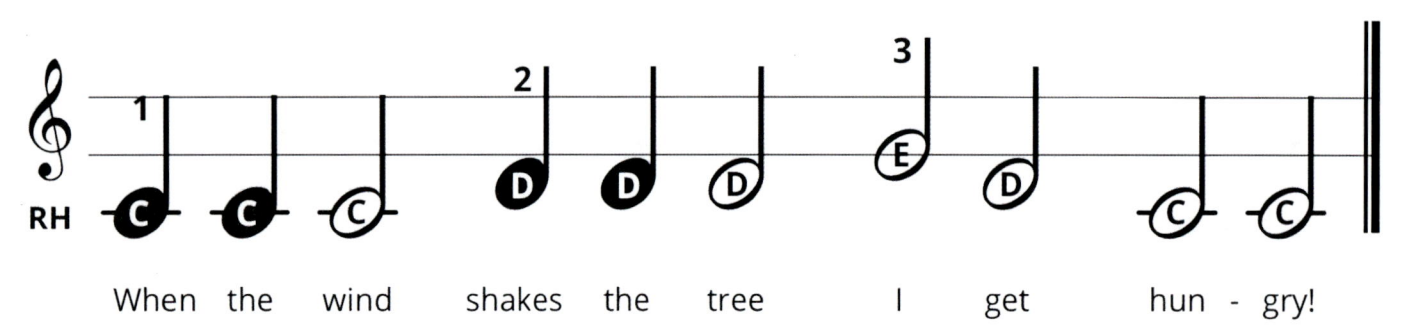

RH: C C C D D D E D C C

When the wind shakes the tree I get hun - gry!

Acorn Pancakes

(Student plays two octaves higher than teacher duet.)

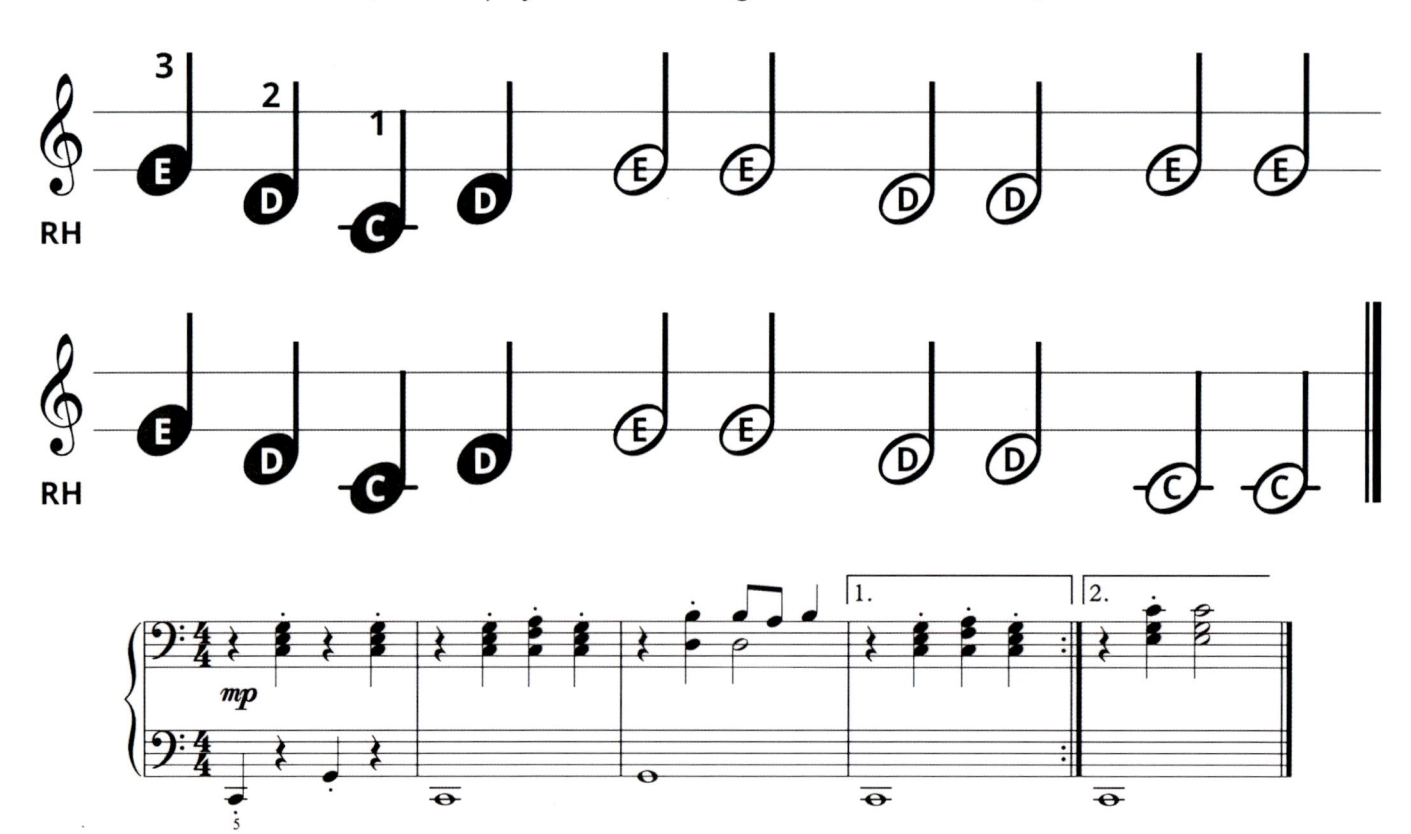

RH: E D C D E E D D E E

RH: E D C D E E D D C C

See reverse for Game Instructions

Aching For Acorns

Aching For Acorns

Game Instructions

Note: The playing cards for *Aching For Acorns* are found at the end of this book.

Players: 2 players

Materials: one laminated game board, 12 coins, 10 playing cards

Game Objectives:

Musical Objective: To reinforce recognition of C, D, and E on the piano
Game Objective: To remove three coins before an opposing player

Setting It Up:

Players should sit beside one another with the game board placed in front and the deck of cards placed between. One coin should be placed over each of the twelve acorns, concealing the letter.

How To Play:

1. To begin, Player 1 removes the top card from the deck and flips it over to reveal an image of a marked piano key.

2. Player 1 determines the name of the marked key and then removes any coin from an acorn image on the game board.

3. If the letter revealed by the coin removed in Step 2 corresponds with the marked key on the back of the card selected in Step 1, Player 1 keeps the coin. If a match is not found, the coin is placed back on the acorn image on the game board.

4. The card selected in Step 1 is removed from the deck and then Player 2 repeats Steps 1 to 3.

5. Players continue alternating turns until one player removes three coins from the game board and wins the game.

6. If all cards have been removed from the deck and a player has not collected three coins, the cards are shuffled and play is continued.

Babysitting Bunny

Hello, Ruby! Who is that hiding behind your leg?

It's my cousin. I'm bunnysitting.

Oh... well, that's okay. Is he able to sit quietly? We have lots to do today. Join us as we learn how to find F, G, A, and B on the piano!

... eleven, twelve, thirteen... Oh, no. I'm missing one!

1. Point to a group of three black keys above. The **white key** below a group of three black keys is F. Color the Fs red. The **white key** to the right of F is G. Color the Gs blue.

2. On the piano, can you play all of the Fs with your LH 5? Can you play all of the Gs with your LH 4?

Babysitting Bunny

You're looking after fourteen baby bunnies?!

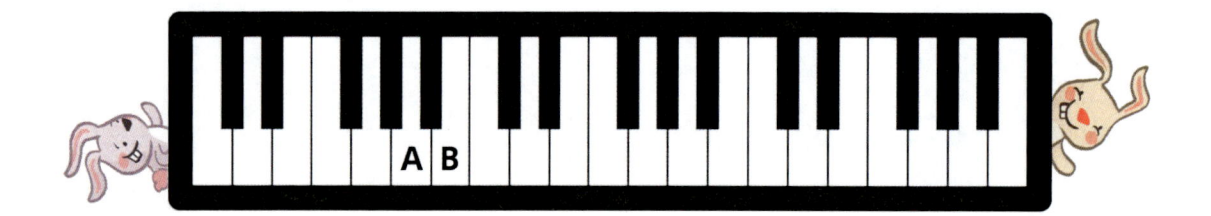

While Ruby counts her cousins, we'll look for A and B. The white key above a group of three black keys is B. On the image above, can you color the Bs red? The white key to the left of B is A. Can you color the As blue? On the piano, play all of the As with your LH 3. Play all of the Bs with your LH 2.

Um, Ruby... I only count twelve babies.

Oops! I'll be right back. The twins like to play hide-and-seek.

Ruby, wait! I can help you find them. I used to do a bit of babysitting myself. Why don't we play a little game?

Let's Help Ruby Find Her Cousins

Thanks for the help! Now I have to get them to bed!

Place your LH 5, 4, 3, and 2 on F, G, A, and B. If I point to a bunny beside an arrow pointing up, play and say, "F-G-A-B". If I point to a bunny beside an arrow pointing down, **play and say**, "B-A-G-F". Let's begin!

F-G-A-B ↗   B-A-G-F ↘   F-G-A-B ↗   B-A-G-F ↘

Babysitting Bunny

Tap each note. Say, "one" when tapping quarter notes and "one-two" when tapping half notes.

I will clap the rhythms below. Can you clap the rhythms back to me?

Place your LH 5, 4, 3, and 2 on F, G, A, and B. I will point to a note. Play its matching key.

Practice On The Pathway

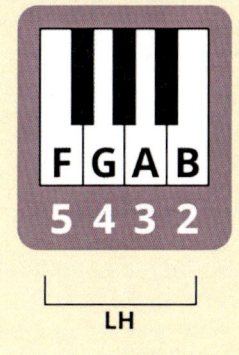

Each Wunder Staff on this page has a **bass clef**. When you see a bass clef, play with your left hand.

Place your LH 5, 4, 3, and 2 on F, G, A, and B. Say the note names as you play.

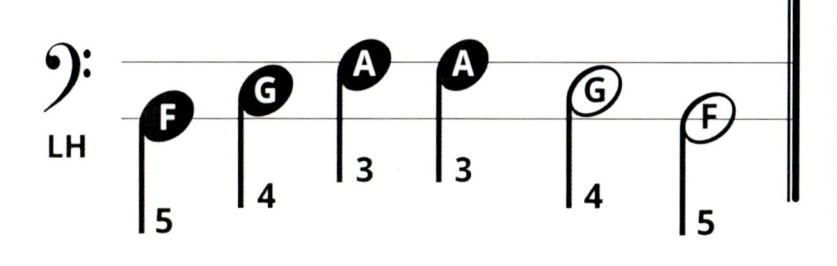

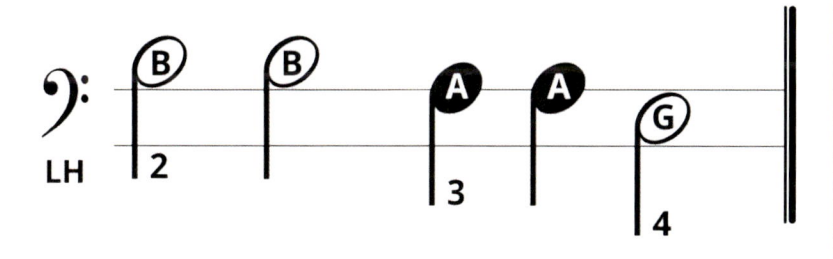

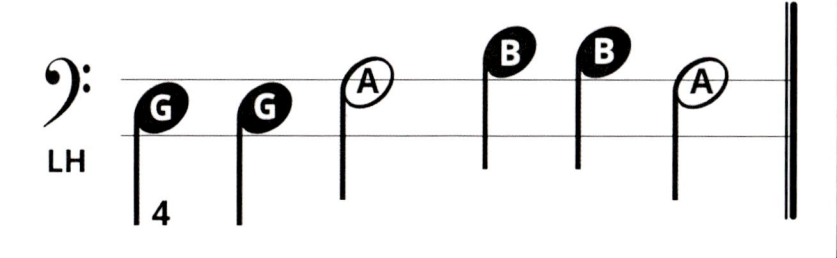

Babysitting Bunny

Phew! I need a break!

Theory Tip: I will point to a bar line on a Wunder Staff below. Bar lines separate music into measures. Count the number of beats in a measure. Count the number of beats in another measure. They have the same number of beats!

Rabbits On The Run

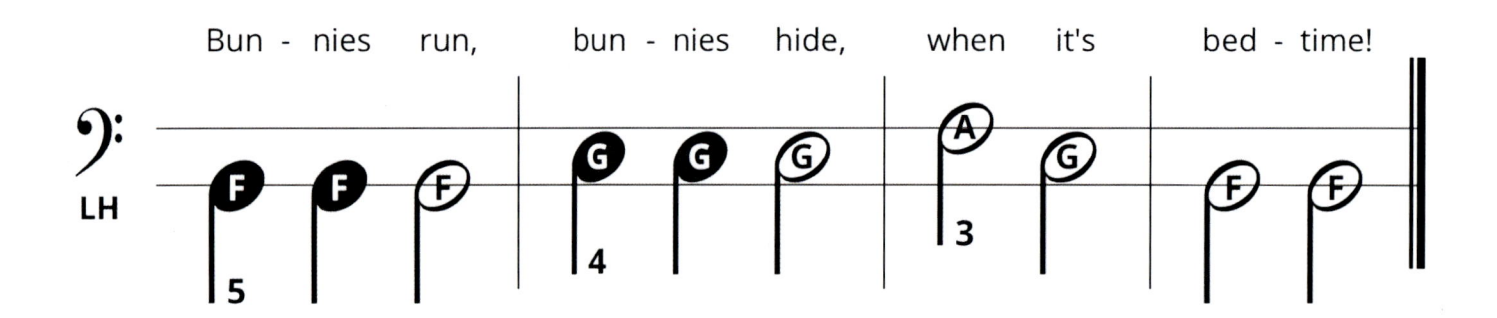

Bun - nies run, bun - nies hide, when it's bed - time!

Bunny Lullabye

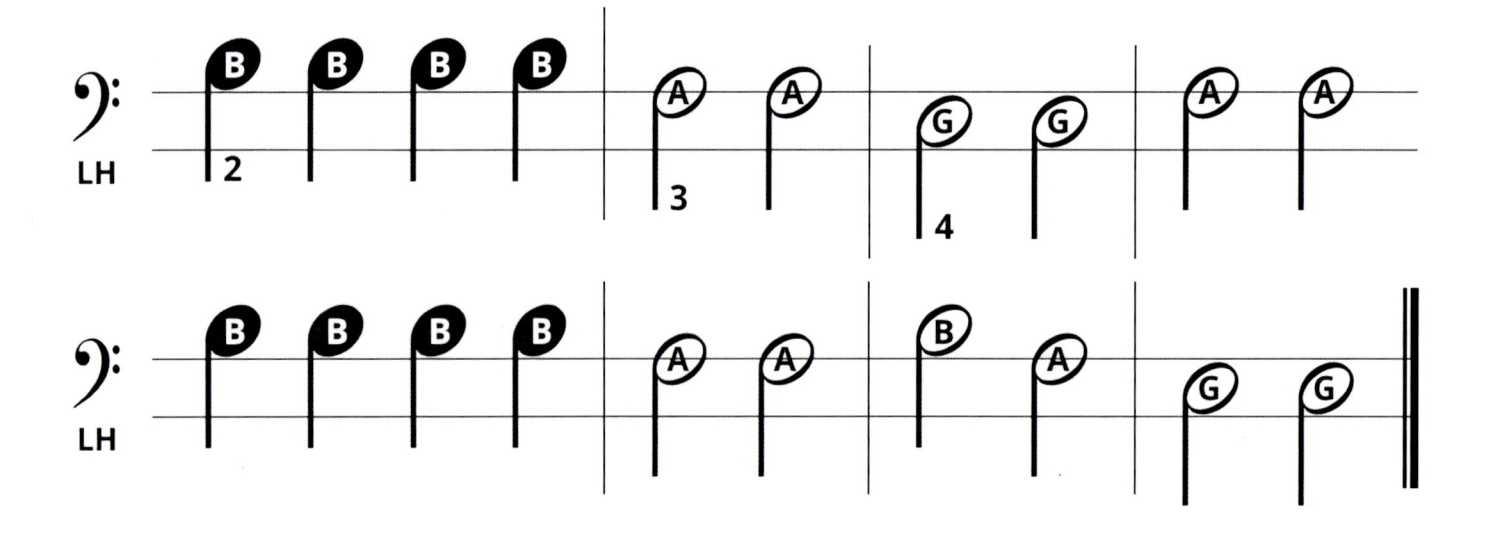

Happy In Hard Hats

Maxine, it's perfectly safe in here. You don't need a hard hat.

We're building a new recital hall. I've been digging all day!

That's wonderful news! Now set your construction equipment aside and join us as we learn something new and exciting.

Building On The Wunder Staff

Using a pencil, trace over the three dashed lines above the Wunder Staff. By adding three lines to the top of a Wunder Staff with a treble clef, you have built a real treble staff. Count the number of lines on the treble staff. Count the number of spaces on the treble staff.

Music notes on the treble staff are played with your right hand. On the treble staff, draw a note in a space. On the treble staff, draw a note on a line.

A Wunder Staff

A Treble Staff

Happy In Hard Hats

Do I see a real bass staff, too?

Maxine spies a bass staff. Do you? Using a pencil, trace over the three dashed lines below the Wunder Staff. By adding three lines to the bottom of a Wunder Staff with a bass clef, you have built a real bass staff. Music notes on the bass staff are played with your left hand. Draw a space note on the bass staff. Draw a line note on the bass staff.

When a bass staff is attached to a treble staff, a **grand staff** is built. Using a grand staff, we can play notes without relying on letter names. **Find the grand staff** at the bottom of this page.

A Wunder Staff

A Bass Staff

Maxine, what is that noise?

Oh no, that's my excavator starting! Gary must be driving!

Oh dear... that is a problem! Just stay for one more moment while we learn our first note on the grand staff.

Middle C On The Grand Staff

1. **Middle C is a line note.** Middle C for RH is on its own line below the treble staff. Its stem is pointing up. Middle C for LH is on its own line above the bass staff. Its stem is pointing down.

2. Use a red crayon to circle the Middle Cs that are played with your right hand and a green crayon to circle the Middle Cs that are played with your left hand.

Happy In Hard Hats

In the practice pieces below, point to each treble staff. Point to each bass staff.

Use your RH 1 to tap the Middle Cs that are played with your right hand.

Use your LH 1 to tap the Middle Cs that are played with your left hand.

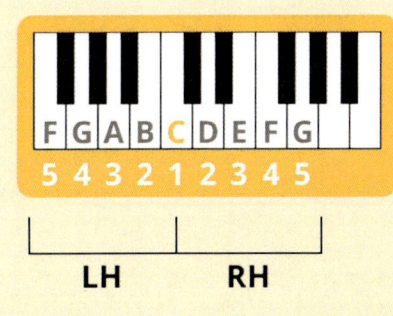

Middle C Position

Let's get your hands ready to play Middle C notes on the grand staff.

On the piano, Middle C is the C closest to the center of the keyboard. Place your RH 1 on Middle C. Rest your RH 2, 3, 4, and 5 fingers on D, E, F, and G. Place your LH 5, 4, 3, 2, and 1 fingers on F, G, A, B, and C. Your thumbs are sharing Middle C!

Now play each practice piece.

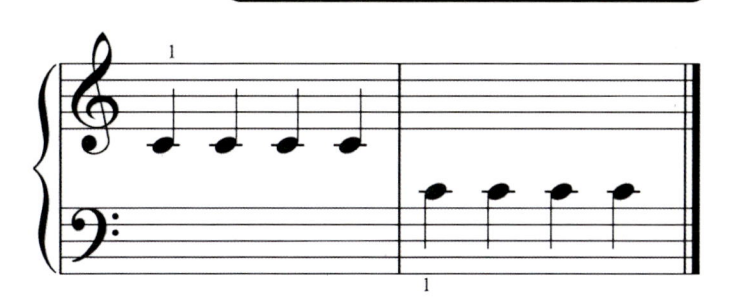

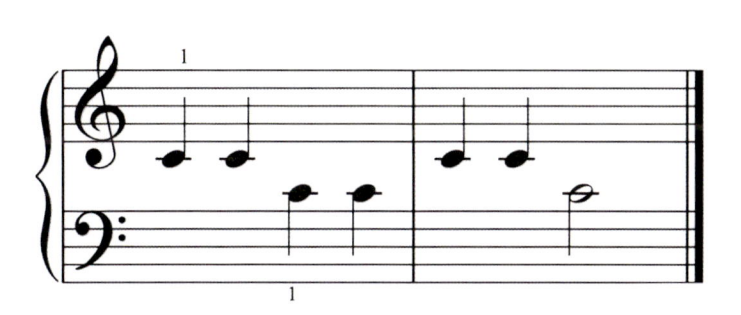

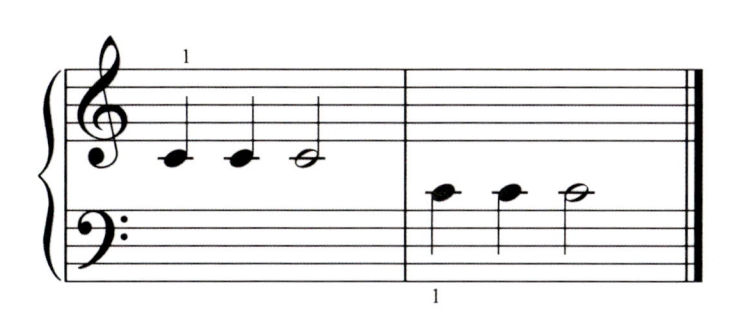

Practice On The Pathway

Happy In Hard Hats

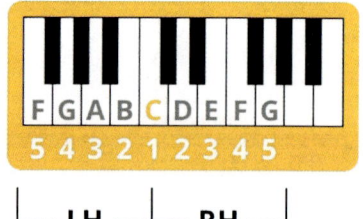

Rock And Roll

I can play rock-in' mu-sic with my fin-gers!

Construction Zone
(Teacher duet below)

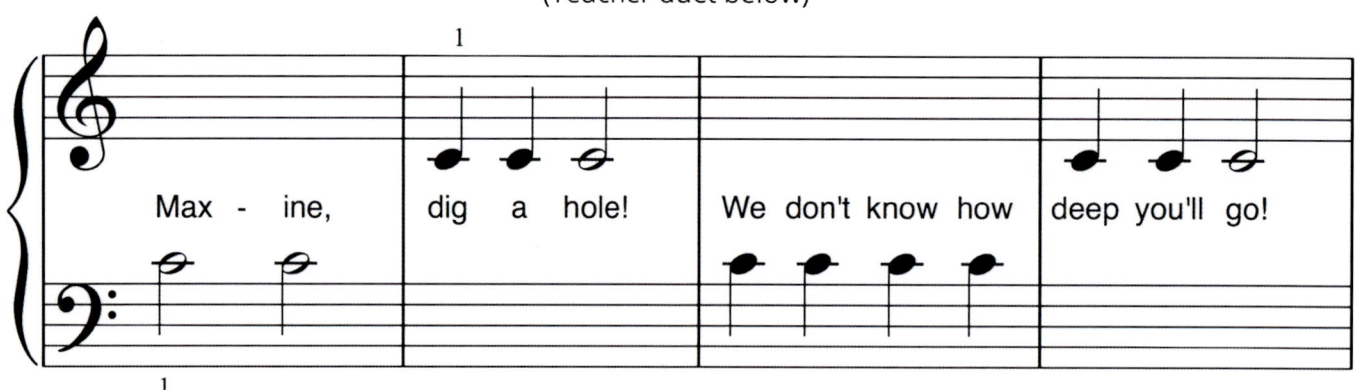

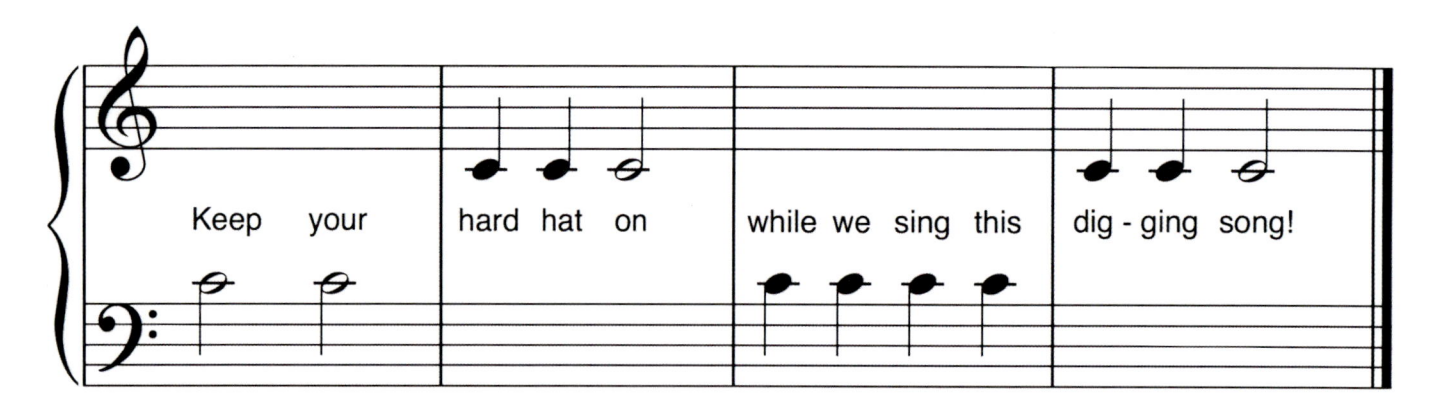

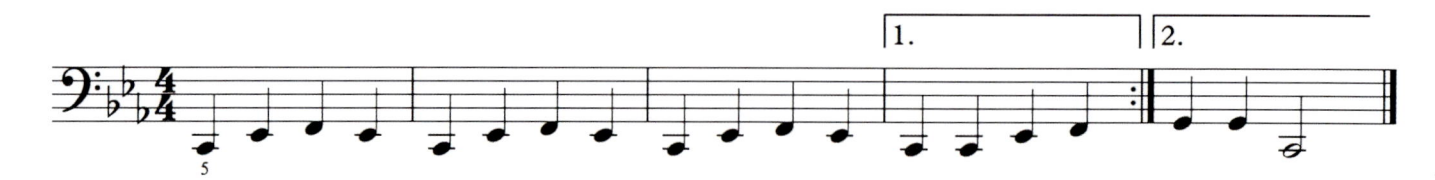

Max-ine, dig a hole! We don't know how deep you'll go!

Keep your hard hat on while we sing this dig-ging song!

See reverse for Game Instructions

Happy In Hard Hats

HAPPY iN Hard Hats

Happy In Hard Hats

Game Instructions

Note: The playing cards for *Happy In Hard Hats* are found at the end of this book.

Players: 2 players

Materials: one laminated game board, eight coins, two dice, five playing cards

Game Objectives:

Musical Objective: To reinforce recognition of Middle C on the grand staff
Game Objective: To move rocks (coins) into or out of the hole

Setting It Up:

Players should sit beside one another with the game board placed in front and the deck of cards placed between. Each player should have a die. Four coins should be placed over rock images inside the hole on the game board, and four coins should be placed over rock images outside the hole on the game board.

How To Play:

1. During the game, the teacher will attempt to move rocks (coins) into the hole and the student will attempt to move rocks (coins) out of the hole.

2. To begin, one player removes the top card from the deck and flips it over to reveal an image of Middle C on the grand staff.

3. At this point the game becomes a race. Step 4 below (while explained for Player 1 only) will be performed simultaneously by both players.

4. As soon as the card in Step 2 is revealed, Player 1 determines if the Middle C on the grand staff should be played with the right hand (treble clef) or the left hand (bass clef) and then attempts to roll a "1" on her die if the Middle C should be played with the right hand or a "2" if the Middle C should be played with the left hand.

5. The first player to roll the correct number on her die wins the round. If the winner is the student, a coin is moved out of the hole and onto the rock stack outside the hole. If the winner is the teacher, a coin is moved from the rock stack outside the hole into the hole.

6. Players repeat Steps 2 to 5 until all five cards have been removed from the deck. At this point the coins inside the hole and outside the hole are counted and then compared. If there are more coins inside the hole, the teacher wins, and if there are more coins outside the hole, the student wins.

Wundertown Baseballers

Hello, Gary! You look like you're ready for a baseball game.

You betcha! I'm the pitcher. Want to see my wind-up?

Whoa! No "winding up" in the studio, Gary! Set your mitt aside and join us as we learn about whole notes.

Home Run Whole Notes

I forgot my pre-game snack. Do you have any honey?

Point to the ball holding a note without a stem. This is a **whole note**. It gets four beats. Count, "one-two-three-four" as I play a whole note.

On a piece of paper, I will draw a baseball diamond with quarter notes on first base and second base, a half note on third base, and a whole note on home plate. Sit down with the paper and ten coins. **Cover any note with a coin**. Listen as I tap a steady beat and play two measures of quarter, half, or whole notes. Remove the coin from its base. If the note under the coin matches the note I played, keep the coin. If not, give the coin to me. Can you collect three coins?

Wundertown Baseballers

"No honey, Gary, but I do have a game!"

"Wahoo, batter up!"

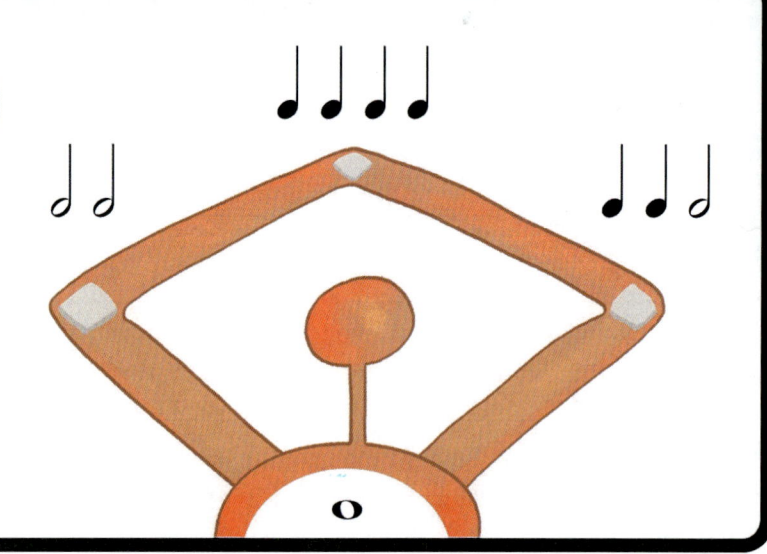

Gary loves baseball. Do you? Run the bases by playing each of the rhythms **on any key**. Next, play the rhythms on Middle C using your RH 1.

"What is that growling noise?"

"It's my tummy. I'm thinking about ballpark hot dogs."

"Try this with us first, Gary, and then you can eat every hot dog at the ballpark!"

Let's Learn About D

1. **D is a space note**. It hangs below the bottom line of the treble staff. On the keyboard, D is the white key to the right of Middle C.

2. Listen as I clap a simple rhythm. Can you play the rhythm back on D? On C?

3. Look at the measure of music to the right. With your hands in Middle C Position, practice stepping between C and D.

Wundertown Baseballers

Is D a space note or a line note? Point to each D in the practice pieces below.

Is Middle C a space note or a line note? Point to each Middle C in the practice pieces.

Can you point to the Middle Cs played with your RH? With your LH?

Practice On The Pathway

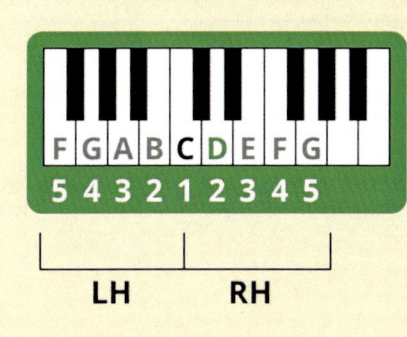

Listen as I clap the rhythms of the practice pieces. Can you clap the rhythms back to me?

Listen and watch as I play each practice piece.

Now it's your turn. Place your hands in Middle C Position. Play each practice piece. Say the note names as you play.

Did you remember to hold the whole notes for four beats?

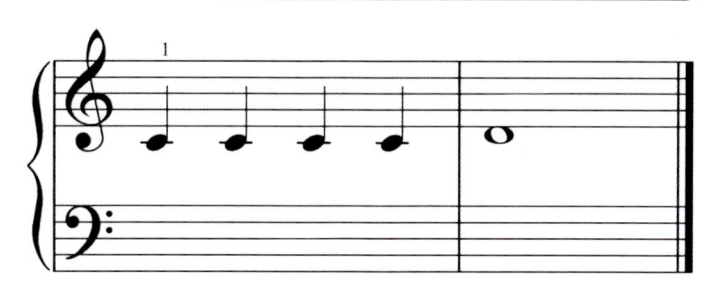

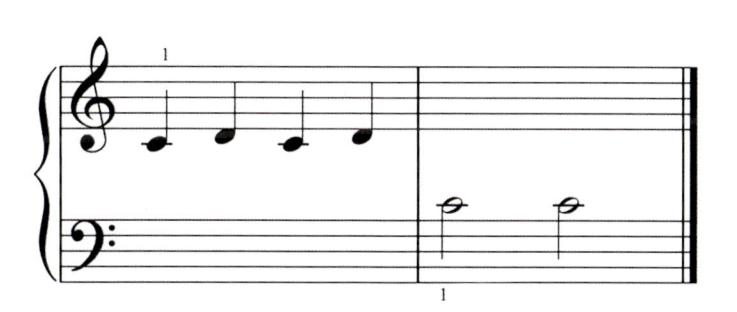

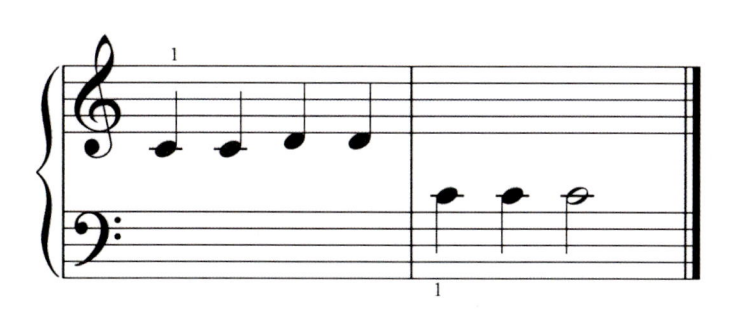

Wundertown Baseballers

My coach told me that I need to step into the pitch. Watch this!

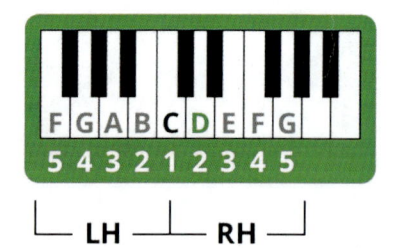

Practice Tip: In music, a step occurs when a line note is followed immediately by a space note or a space note is followed immediately by a line note. Can you find steps in the music below? To play a step on the keyboard we move from one white key to the very next white key. Can you play a step on the keyboard?

Batter Up

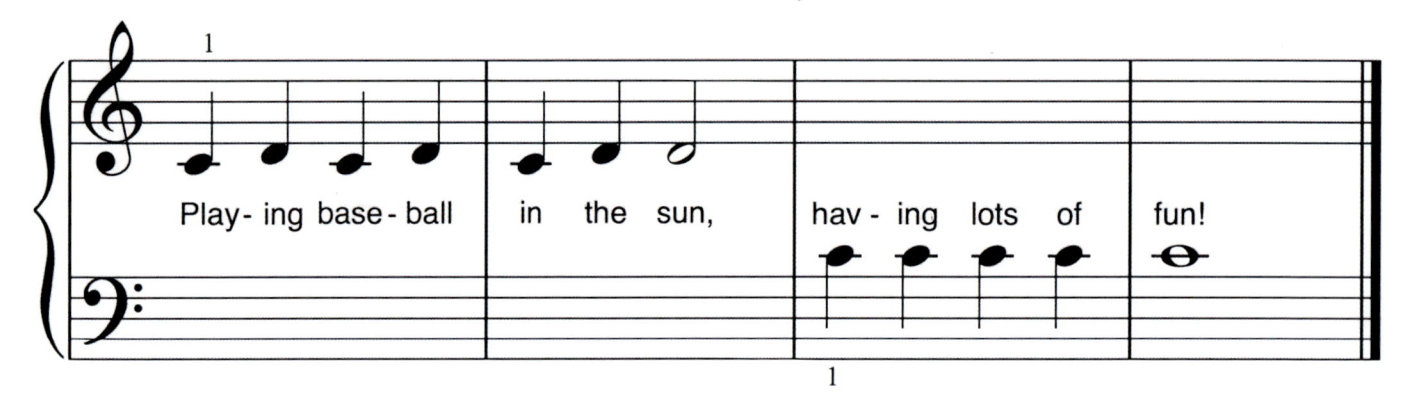

Play- ing base - ball | in the sun, | hav- ing lots of | fun!

'Round The Bases

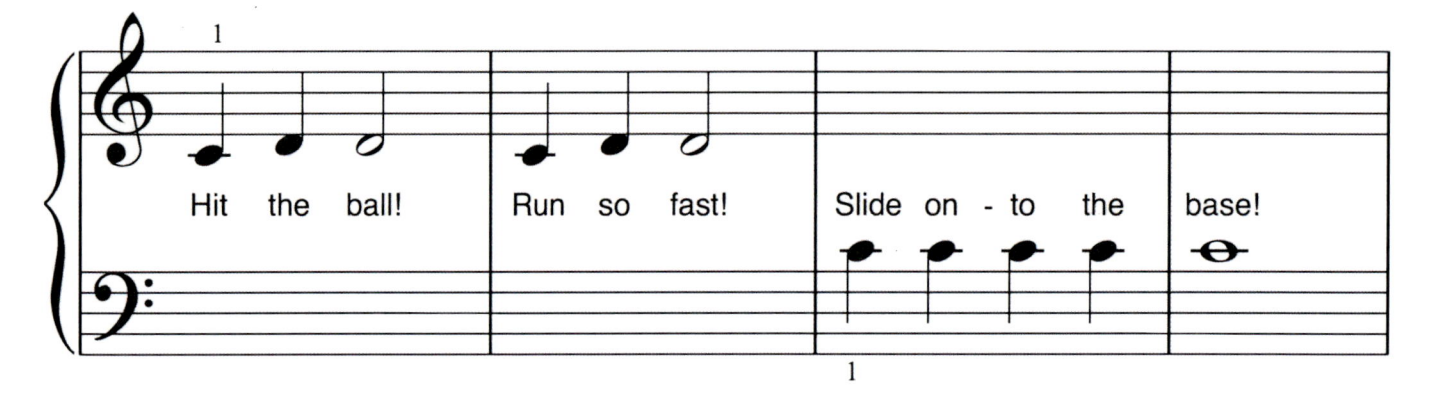

Hit the ball! | Run so fast! | Slide on - to the | base!

Bat - ter, | here's the pitch! | 'Round the field you | race!

Flying Squirrel

Sheldon, did you just parachute into my yard?

Yes, I did! I'm taking Flying Squirrel lessons.

But I don't think you are a flying squirr- *sigh.* Never mind. Strap on that parachute again and join us as we jump into more bass staff fun.

Let's Learn About B

1. **B is a space note** that sits above the top line of the bass staff. On the keyboard, B is the white key to the left of Middle C.

2. Listen as I clap a simple rhythm. Can you play the rhythm back on B? On C?

3. Look at the measure of music to the right. With your hands in Middle C Position, practice stepping between B and C.

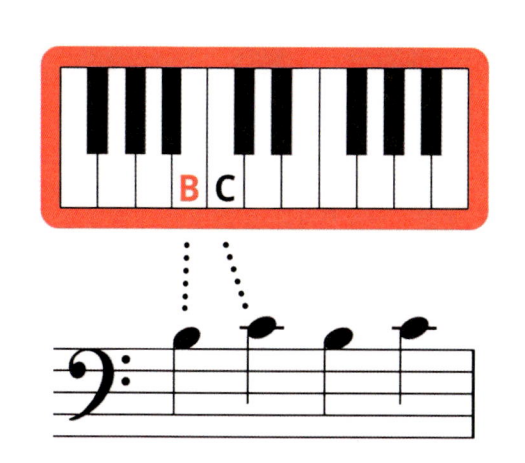

Flying Squirrel

"Look at this! Run, run, run... leap!"

"Sheldon, I'll give you an acorn if you come down!"

While we're waiting for Sheldon, look at the music below. Point to the Bs. Point to the Middle Cs. Circle the notes that **repeat**. With your hands in Middle C Position, use your LH 2 and 1 to play the piece below.

"You look like you have an idea."

"From up in the air I noticed that B looks like a bunny peeking out of its hole."

"Ruby said the same thing! Remember D from last lesson? It looks like a dog "digging a hole" below the staff. Let's practice reading Bs and Ds."

Let's Help Sheldon With B And D

"Time to fly, Sheldon!"

Inside the circles below are Bs and Ds. Can you use the "peeking bunny" and "digging dog" tricks to name the notes in the circles? **Using a pencil**, draw "sticking up" bunny ears on the circles holding Bs and "flopping down" dog ears on the circles holding Ds.

Flying Squirrel

In the practice pieces below, draw a red circle around a D and a green circle around a B.

Find two notes that are repeating. Draw a red line above the notes.

Find two notes that are stepping. Draw a green line connecting the note heads.

Practice On The Pathway

F G A **B** C D E F G
5 4 3 2 1 2 3 4 5
LH — RH

Listen as I clap the rhythms of the practice pieces. Can you clap the rhythms back to me?

These pieces have **repeat signs**... double bar lines with two dots. When you see a repeat sign in your music, return to the beginning and play the piece again.

Listen and watch as I play each practice piece. Now it's your turn. Place your hands in Middle C Position and make some music! Say the note names as you play.

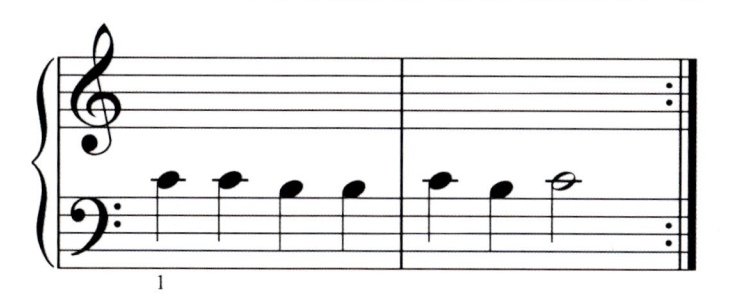

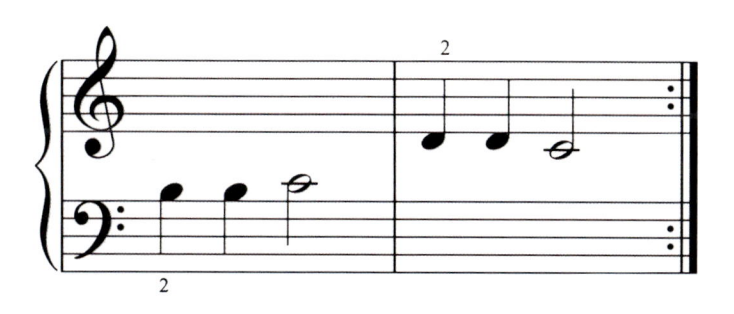

Flying Squirrel

Glide On By

I can fly | in the sky. | I'm a fly-ing squir-rel!

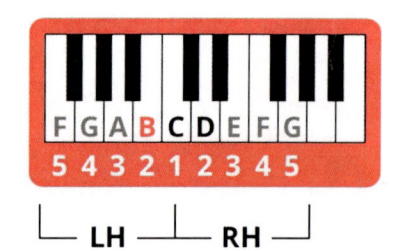

Flying Fur
(Teacher duet below)

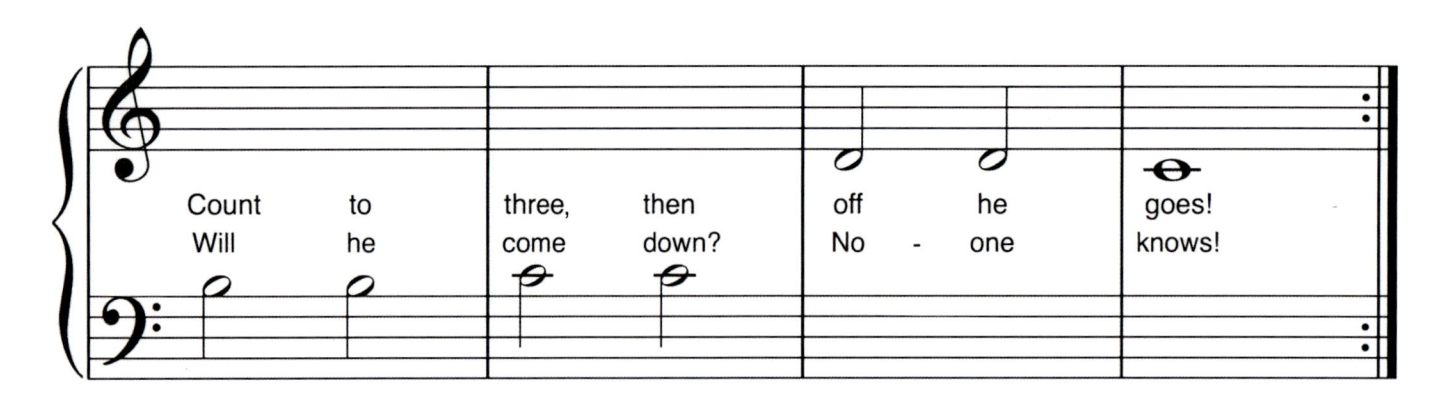

1. Shel-don's heart starts | thump-ing | when it's time for | jump-ing!
2. Par-a-chute is | op-en, | Shel-don is a | float-in'!

Count to | three, then | off he | goes!
Will he | come down? | No-one | knows!

See reverse for Game Instructions

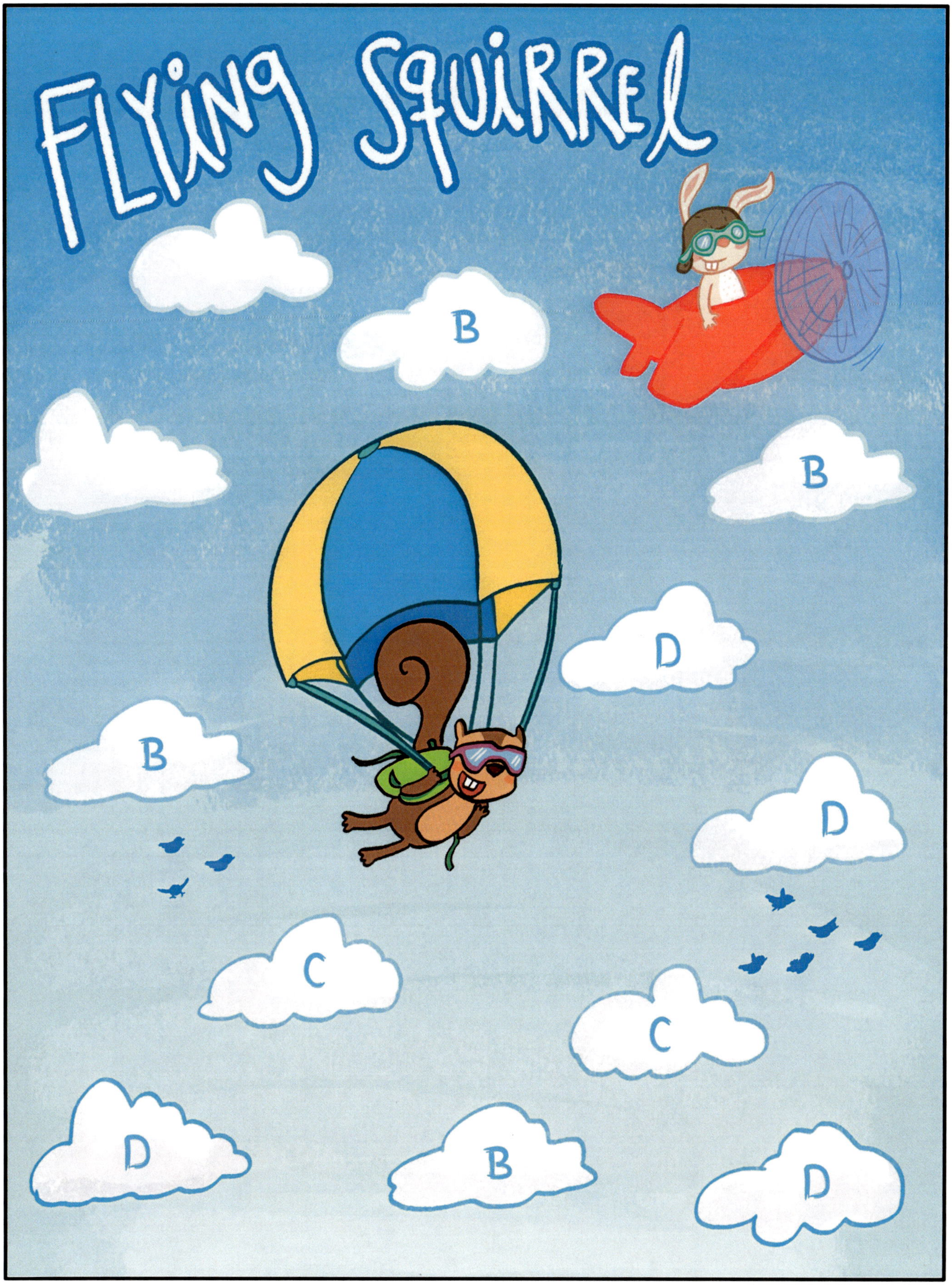

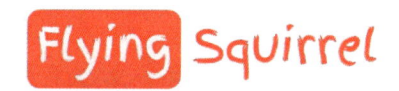

Flying Squirrel

Game Instructions

Note: The playing cards for *Flying Squirrel* are found at the end of this book.

Players: 2 players

Materials: one laminated game board, 10 playing cards, 10 pennies, 10 dimes, two dice

Game Objectives:

Musical Objective: To reinforce recognition of B, Middle C, and D on the grand staff
Game Objective: To place more coins over cloud images than an opposing player

Setting It Up:

Players should sit beside one another with the game board placed in front and the deck of cards placed to the side. Player 1 should have a die and ten pennies. Player 2 should have a die and ten dimes.

How To Play:

1. To begin, either player removes the top card from the deck and flips it over to reveal an image of a note on the grand staff accompanied by a number.

2. At this point the game becomes a race with each player rolling her die in attempt to have it display a value that corresponds to the number revealed on the card in Step 1. The first player to roll the matching value wins the round.

3. The player winning the round names the note on the card revealed in Step 1 and places one coin over any cloud displaying a note name that matches the note image on the card.

4. Players repeat Steps 1 to 3 until all cards have been removed from the deck.

5. At this point the game is over and the player with the most coins on the game board wins the game.

Big Air Bunny

Did you land a backflip while holding that carrot?

Nope! This is my post-ride reward... from your garden.

From my garden?! *Sigh.* If you took just one, I should have enough carrots left for a cake. Now, join us as we learn to read "E" on the treble staff.

Let's Learn About E

1. **E is a line note.** It is on the bottom line of the treble staff. On the keyboard, E is the white key to the right of D.

2. Listen as I clap a simple rhythm. Can you play the rhythm back on E? On D? On C?

3. Look at the measure of music to the right. With your hands in Middle C Position, say the note names as you play.

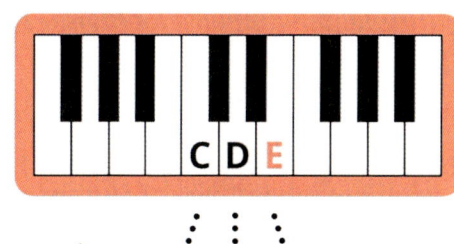

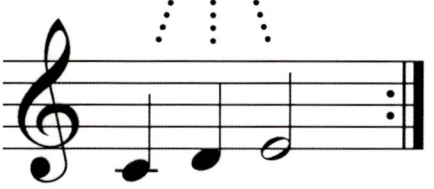

Big Air Bunny

Riding The Ramp

Can you ride like Ruby? Stand in the middle of the room. If you hear me play: 1) notes stepping up, jump forward, 2) notes stepping down, jump backward, and 3) repeating notes, jump in place.

In the music below, **circle notes** that are: 1) stepping up with a red crayon, 2) stepping down with a blue crayon, and 3) repeating with a green crayon. Using your RH 1, 2, and 3, play the excerpt below on C, D, and E.

> Stepping up and down on the keys is like riding on a bike ramp.

> Yes, but when I'm biking there's usually a cheering crowd.

> That sounds thrilling! Dynamic markings in your piano pieces can make music exciting, too. Let's learn about forte and piano.

f = forte (loud) p = piano (soft)

I am going to point to a wheel on Ruby's bike. Play a loud sound on a key if the dynamic marking inside the wheel is an f. Play a soft sound on a key if the dynamic marking inside the wheel is a p.

> I'll grab a carrot for the road. You may want to plant more!

Big Air Bunny

In the practice pieces below, find notes that step up, step down, and repeat.

Can you point to the notes that are played with your RH? With your LH?

In the practice pieces, tap each note and say its name. How many Es did you tap?

Practice On The Pathway

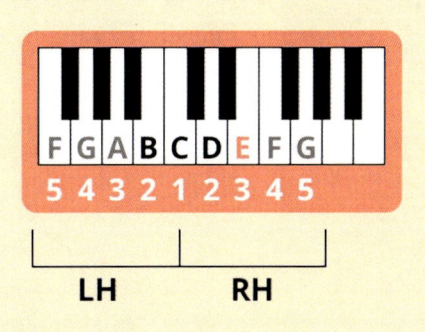

F G A B C D E F G
5 4 3 2 1 2 3 4 5
LH   RH

Listen as I clap the rhythms of the practice pieces. Can you clap the rhythms back to me?

Listen and watch as I play each practice piece.

Now it's your turn! Place your hands in Middle C Position and make some music.

Did you remember to play the second practice piece loudly? Did you remember to play the third practice piece softly?

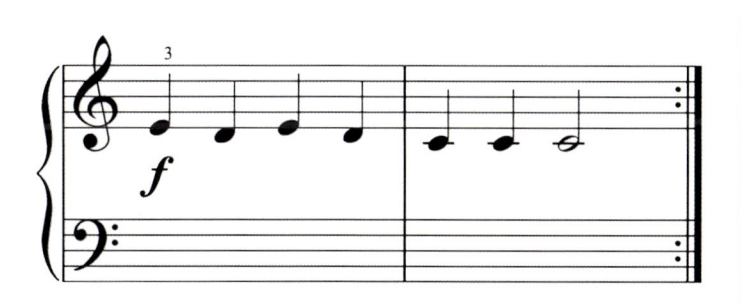

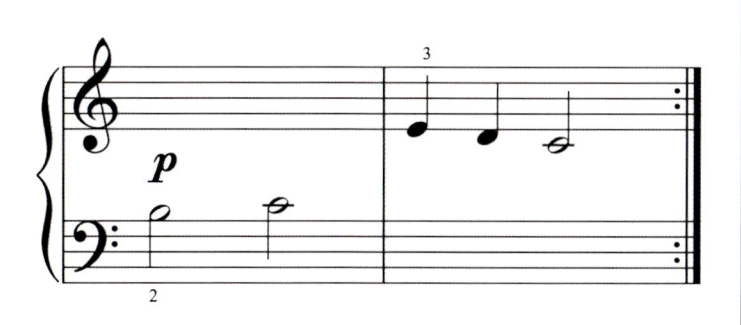

Big Air Bunny

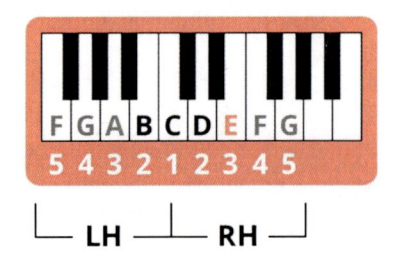

Practice Tip: Before playing the piano pieces below, look for notes that are stepping up, stepping down, and repeating.

Air Trick

f
1. Ped - al fast up the hill! Ru - by does a back - flip!
2. She can show off her skills do - ing lots of bike tricks!

Bunny Hop

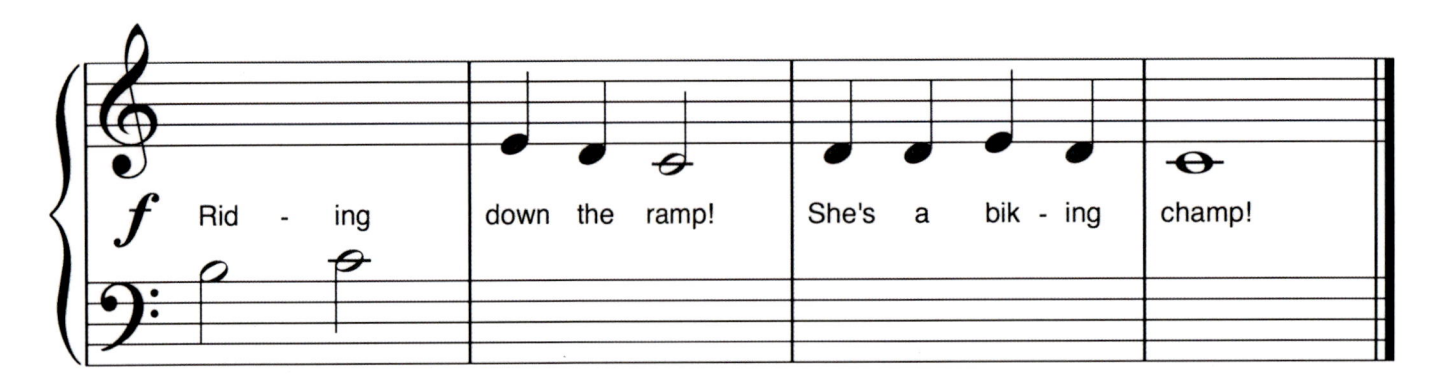

p Rid - ing rab - bit style! Rid - ing with a smile!

f Rid - ing down the ramp! She's a bik - ing champ!

Campfire Cookout

You look worried, Maxine. Is something the matter?

We're going camping tonight and I haven't slept in a tent before.

Oh, Maxine, if Gary is there you'll be perfectly safe. His snoring will keep anything scary away! Now join us as we learn about A.

Let's Learn About A

1. **A is a line note.** It is on the top line of the bass staff. On the keyboard, A is the white key to the left of B.

2. Listen as I clap a simple rhythm. Can you play the rhythm back on A? On B? On C?

3. Look at the measure of music to the right. With your hands in Middle C Position, say the note names as you play.

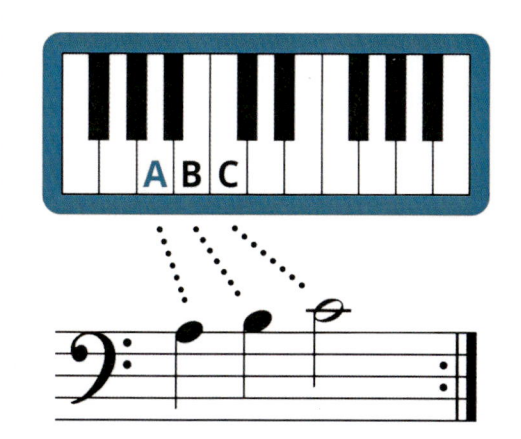

Campfire Cookout

Let's Help Maxine With Marshmallows

"Oh, no! A looks a lot like E."

Draw a line from each note name pattern to its matching grand staff. Then, with your hands in Middle C Position, play each measure.

E A A A

E A E E

E E A E

"Maxine, why do you still look worried?"

"Do you think Ruby, Sheldon, AND Gary will fit in a four-person tent with me?"

"Of course! The four of you will fit like four beats in a measure. Oooh, that reminds me..."

Help me teach Maxine about 4/4 time. A time signature is found at the start of a piano piece. In 4/4 time, the top 4 means that each measure in a piece has four beats. The bottom 4 means a quarter note gets one beat. Let's clap and count the rhythms below to wake up Gary! Next, play and count the rhythms on any key.

1 2 3 4 | 1-2 3-4

1 2 3-4 | 1-2-3-4

Campfire Cookout

The practice pieces below are in 4/4 time. Clap and count each piece.

Find notes in the music that are stepping up, stepping down, and repeating.

In the practice pieces, tap each note and say its name. How many As did you tap?

Practice On The Pathway

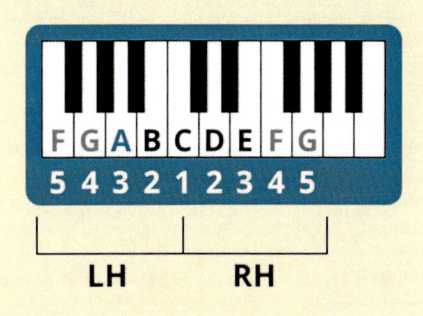

F G A B C D E F G
5 4 3 2 1 2 3 4 5
LH   RH

Listen as I clap the rhythms of the practice pieces. Can you clap the rhythms back to me?

Listen and watch as I play each practice piece.

Now it's your turn! Place your hands in Middle C Position and make some music.

Did you remember to play the second practice piece softly? Did you remember to play the third practice piece loudly?

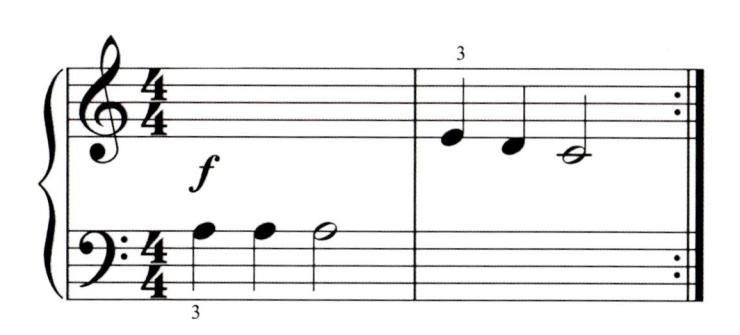

Campfire Cookout

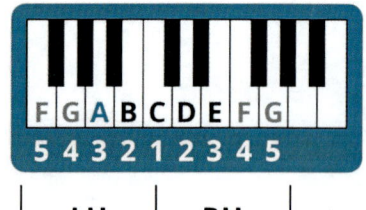

Gary's Lullaby

1. If the night-time's scar-y, find a friend like Ga-ry.
2. He will keep you coz-y when you're feel-ing do-zy!

'Til Morning Comes
(Teacher duet below)

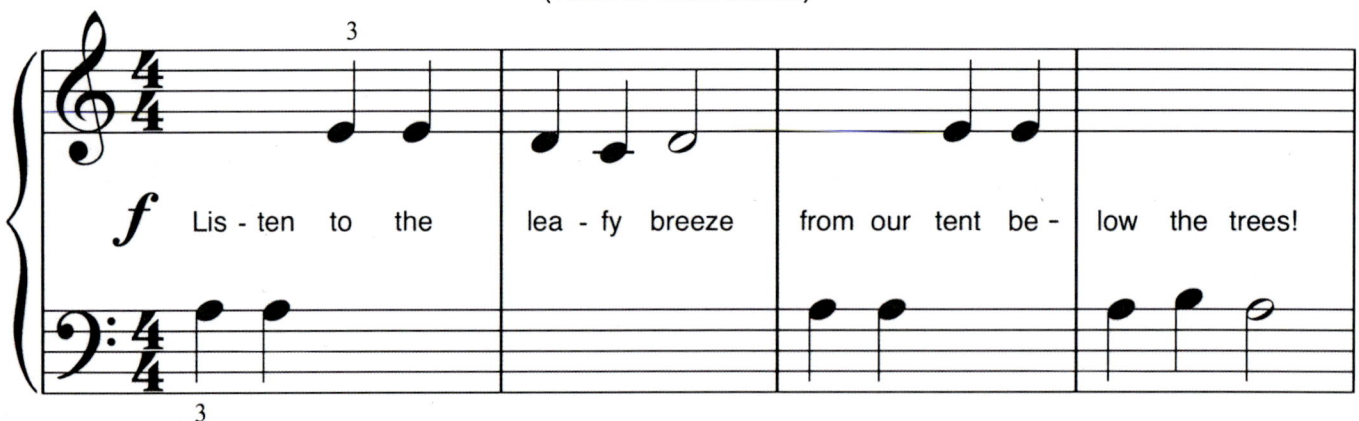

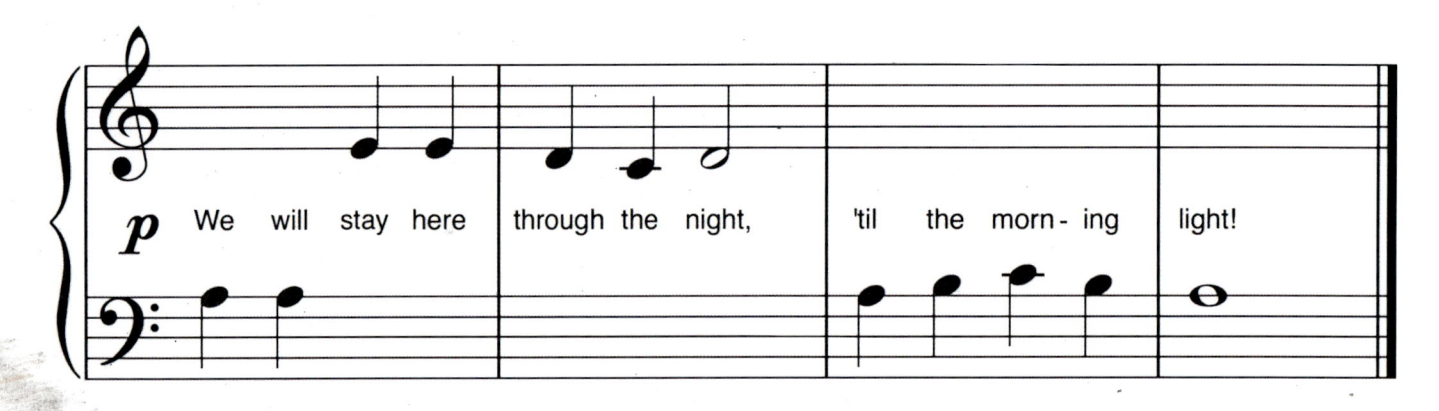

Lis-ten to the lea-fy breeze from our tent be-low the trees!

We will stay here through the night, 'til the morn-ing light!

See reverse for Game Instructions

Campfire Cookout

CAMPFIRE COOKOUT

Campfire Cookout

Game Instructions

Note: The playing cards for *Campfire Cookout* are found at the end of this book.

Players: 2 players

Materials: one game board, five playing cards, two game markers, two dice, 12 coins

Game Objectives:

Musical Objective: To reinforce visual recognition of stepping and repeating notes
Game Objective: To collect more coins (marshmallows) than an opposing player

Setting It Up:

Players should sit beside one another with the game board placed in front and the deck of cards placed to the side. Each player should have a die. Player 1 should place his game marker on the log marked with a "1," and Player 2 should place her game marker on the log marked with a "2."

How To Play:

1. On the count of three, either player flips over the top card of the deck to reveal stepping or repeating notes.

2. At this point the game becomes a race. Step 3 is described for Player 1 only but will be performed by both players simultaneously.

3. Player 1 determines (on his own) if the notes displayed on the card revealed in Step 1 represent notes stepping up, notes stepping down, or notes repeating, and then attempts to roll a "1" on his die if they represent notes stepping up, a "2" on his die if they represent notes stepping down, or a "3" on his die if they represent notes repeating.

4. The first player to roll the correct number wins the round.

5. The player winning the round rolls his die again and moves his game marker clockwise around the game board according to the number rolled. If his game marker lands on an empty log, his turn is over. If his game marker lands on a character, he collects one coin and his turn is over. *Note: The empty logs and the characters sitting on logs are all considered game squares that a marker must move along.*

6. When all cards are removed from the deck, they are shuffled and play is continued.

7. Players repeat Steps 1 to 6 until one player collects **three coins** and wins the game.

Double Decker Delight

"Oh! You're all here. I was only expecting Gary!"

"We're leaving for London and wanted to say goodbye."

"Gary, I think you're squeezing too tight! Put your friends down and we'll learn a new time signature before you go."

Let's Teach The Friends A New Time Signature

This is a **3/4 time signature**. The top 3 means each measure has three beats. The bottom 4 means the quarter note gets one beat.

Clap and count, "one-two-three" or "one-two-three-four" for each rhythm on the right. Complete the time signatures by writing a "3" or a "4" in the circles.

Double Decker Delight

"Oh no! Whole notes won't fit in 3/4 time."

Maxine is right... but a dotted half note will! A **dotted half note** gets three beats.

Using a pencil, add a dot to the half notes below to turn them into dotted half notes. Tap each one as you count, "one-two-three."

"Hmm... Those dots look like bees. That reminds me..."

"...we need honey for the plane ride."

"No, not honey, Gary... Carrots!"

"WALNuts!"

"I'm sure they'll have all sorts of snacks on the plane. But first, let's play a game before you go."

Load The Bus, It's Adventure Time!

1. Stand on the side of the room opposite the door. I will clap and count a two-measure rhythm in 4/4 or 3/4 time.

2. **Name the time signature** of the clapped rhythm. If you are correct and the rhythm was in 3/4 time, hop forward three times. If you are correct and the rhythm was in 4/4 time, hop forward four times. If you are incorrect, stay where you are.

3. Let's play until you reach the door and board the bus.

"CHEERIO! We have a plane to catch."

Double Decker Delight

Clap and count the practice pieces below. Don't forget to look for the time signatures.

Use your LH 3 to tap all the As. Use your RH 3 to tap all the Es.

Find notes in the music that are stepping up, stepping down, and repeating.

Practice On The Pathway

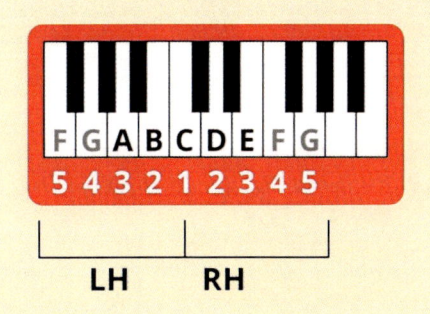

Listen as I clap the rhythms of the practice pieces. Can you clap the rhythms back to me?

Listen and watch as I play each practice piece.

Now it's your turn! Place your hands in Middle C Position and make some music.

Did you remember to play the second practice piece loudly? Did you remember to play the third practice piece softly?

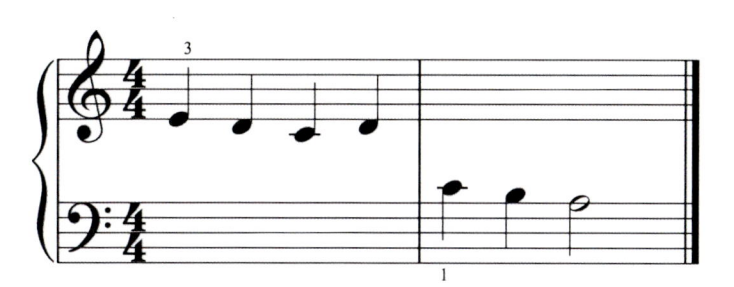

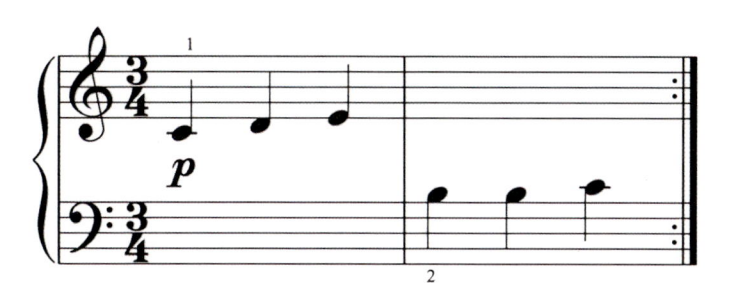

Double Decker Delight

Practice Tip: Clap and count the rhythm of each piece. Look at the time signature before you clap and count.

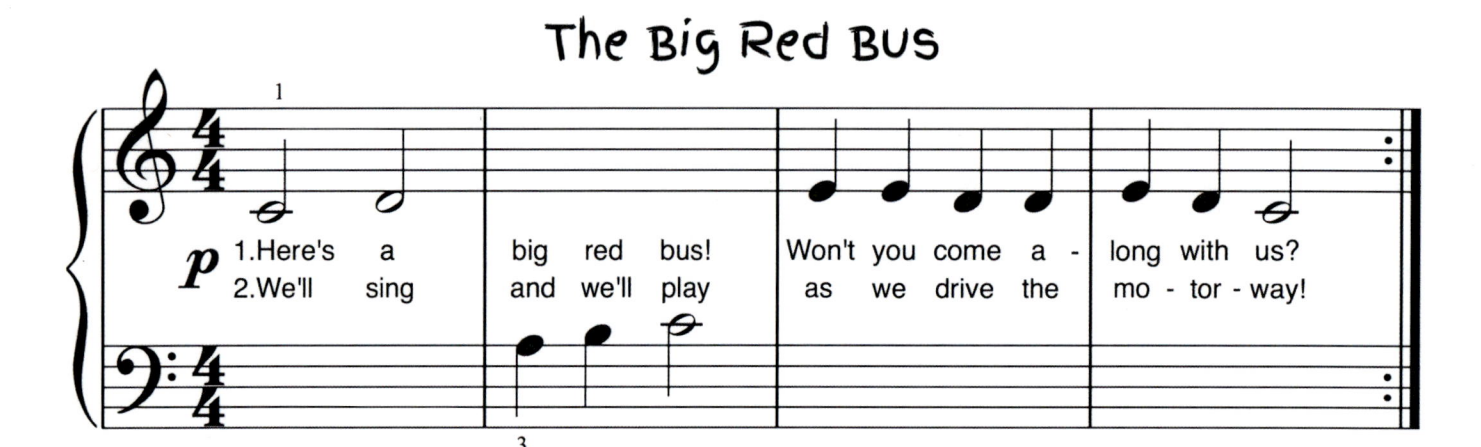

The Big Red Bus

1. Here's a big red bus! Won't you come a-long with us?
2. We'll sing and we'll play as we drive the mo-tor-way!

London Bound

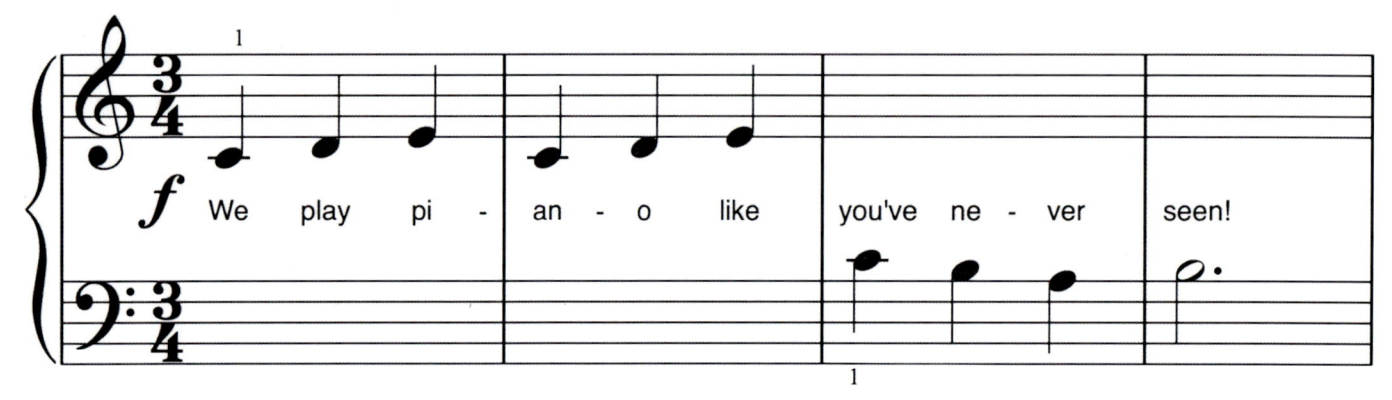

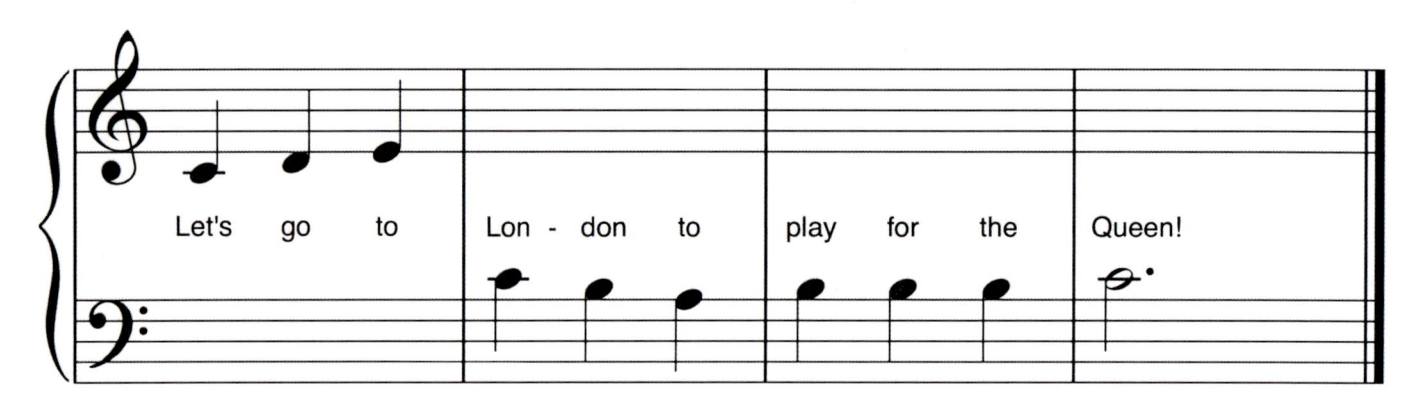

We play pi-an-o like you've ne-ver seen!

Let's go to Lon-don to play for the Queen!

Cut and laminate the card sets below.

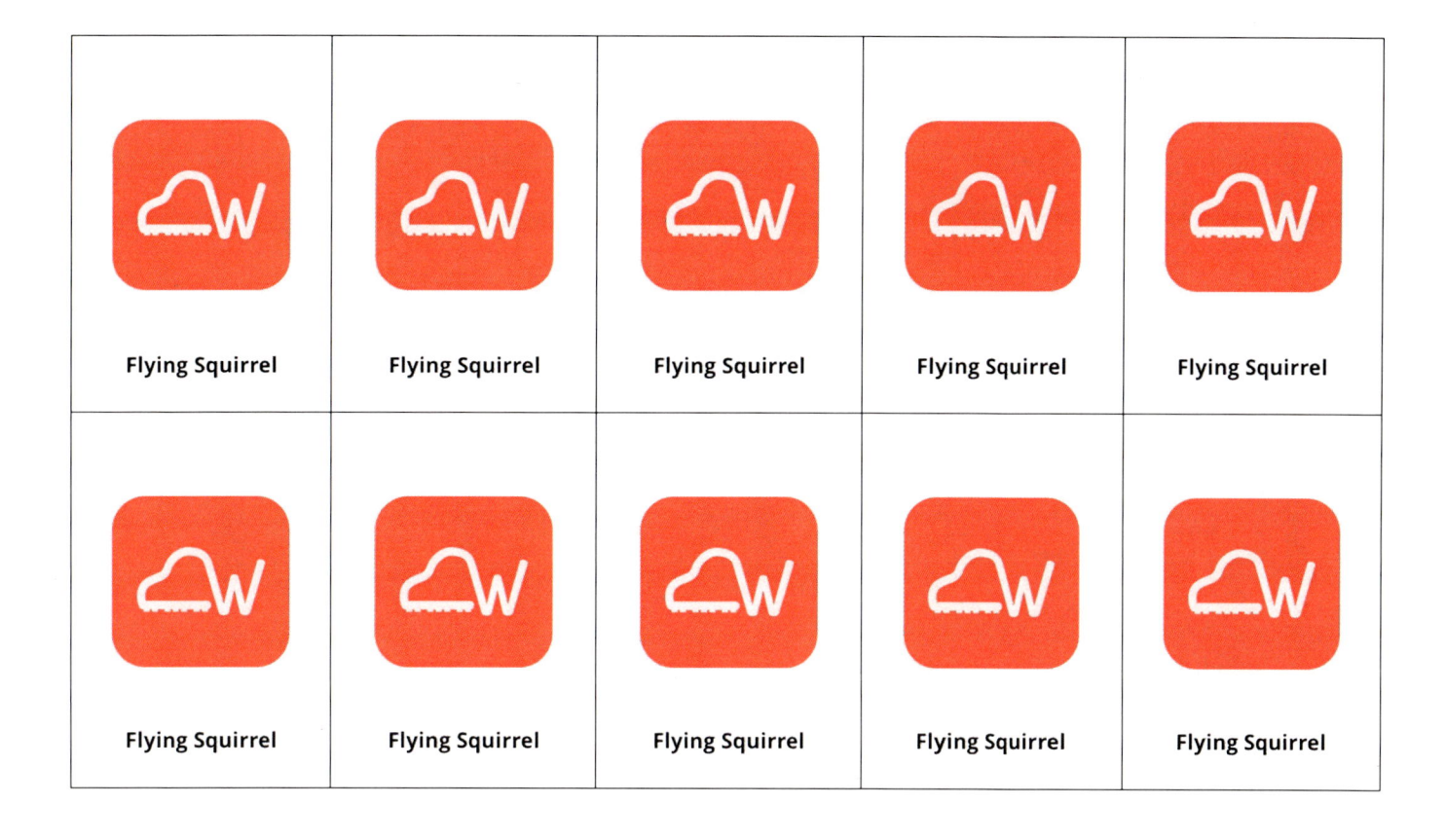

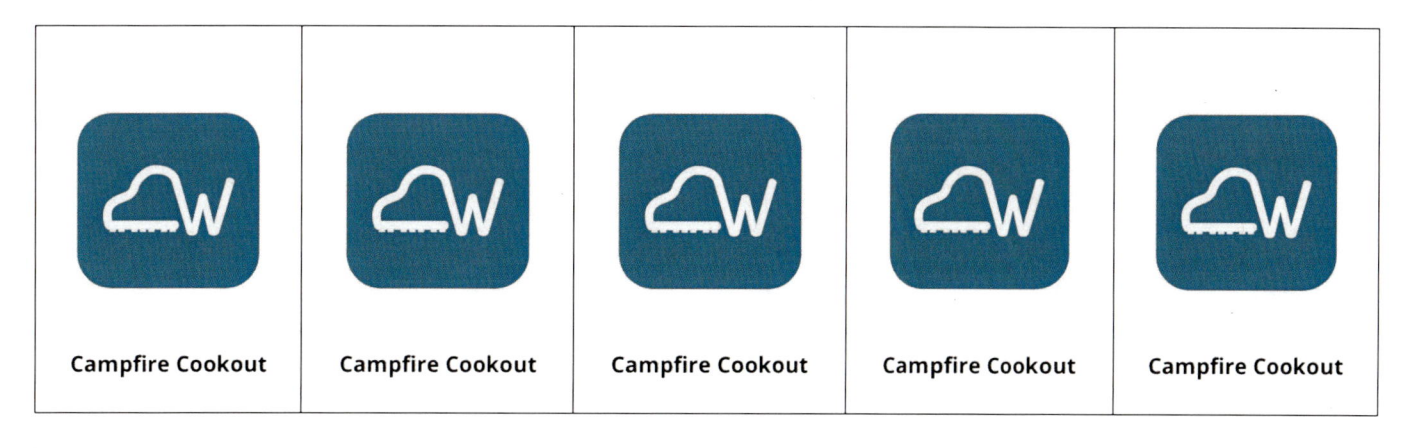

WunderKeys Card Sets

| Happy In Hard Hats | Happy In Hard Hats | Happy In Hard Hats | Happy In Hard Hats | Happy In Hard Hats |

| Flying Squirrel | Flying Squirrel | Flying Squirrel | Flying Squirrel | Flying Squirrel |

| Flying Squirrel | Flying Squirrel | Flying Squirrel | Flying Squirrel | Flying Squirrel |

| Campfire Cookout | Campfire Cookout | Campfire Cookout | Wumpfire Cookout | Campfire Cookout |

WunderKeys Card Sets

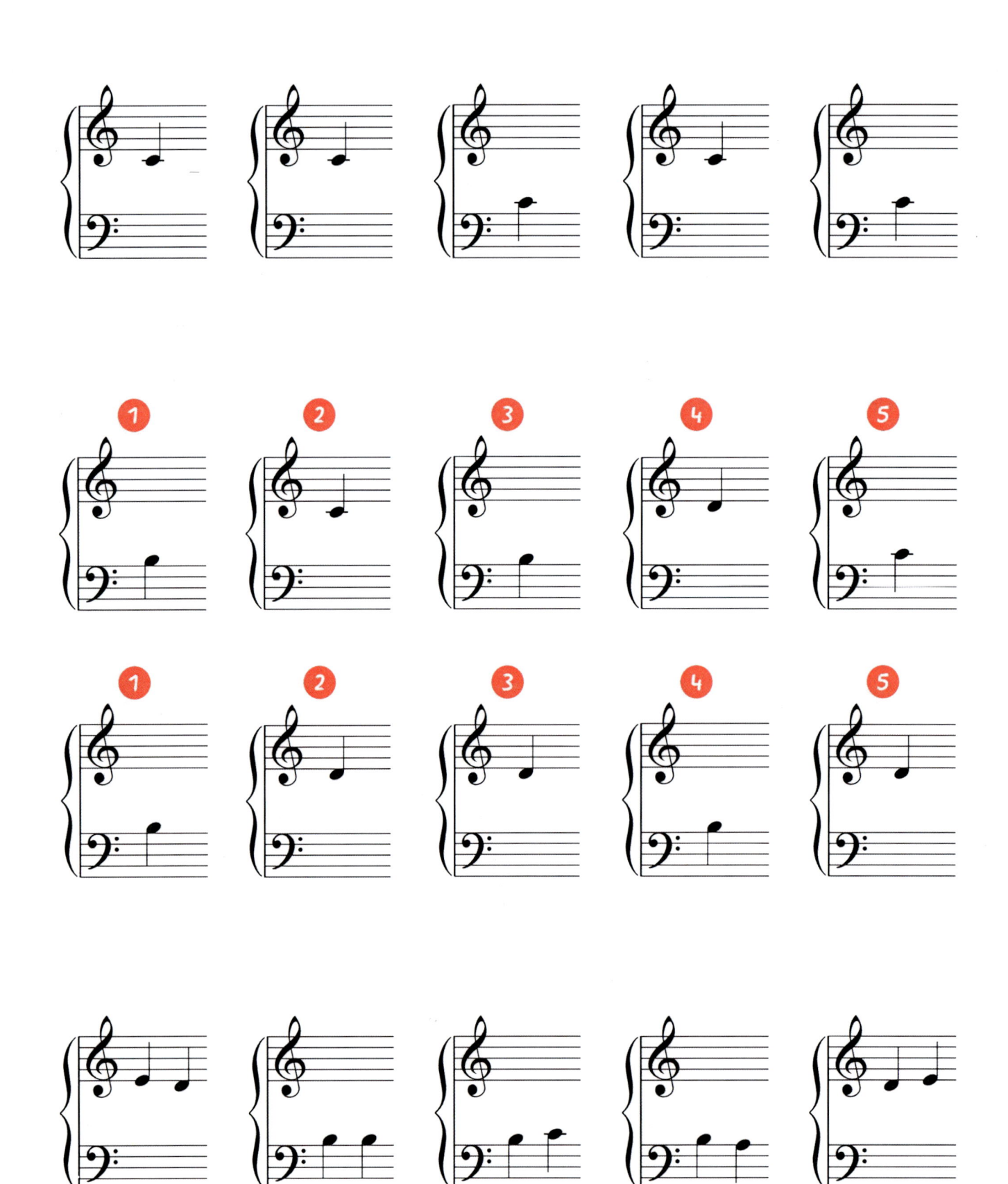

Certificate of Completion

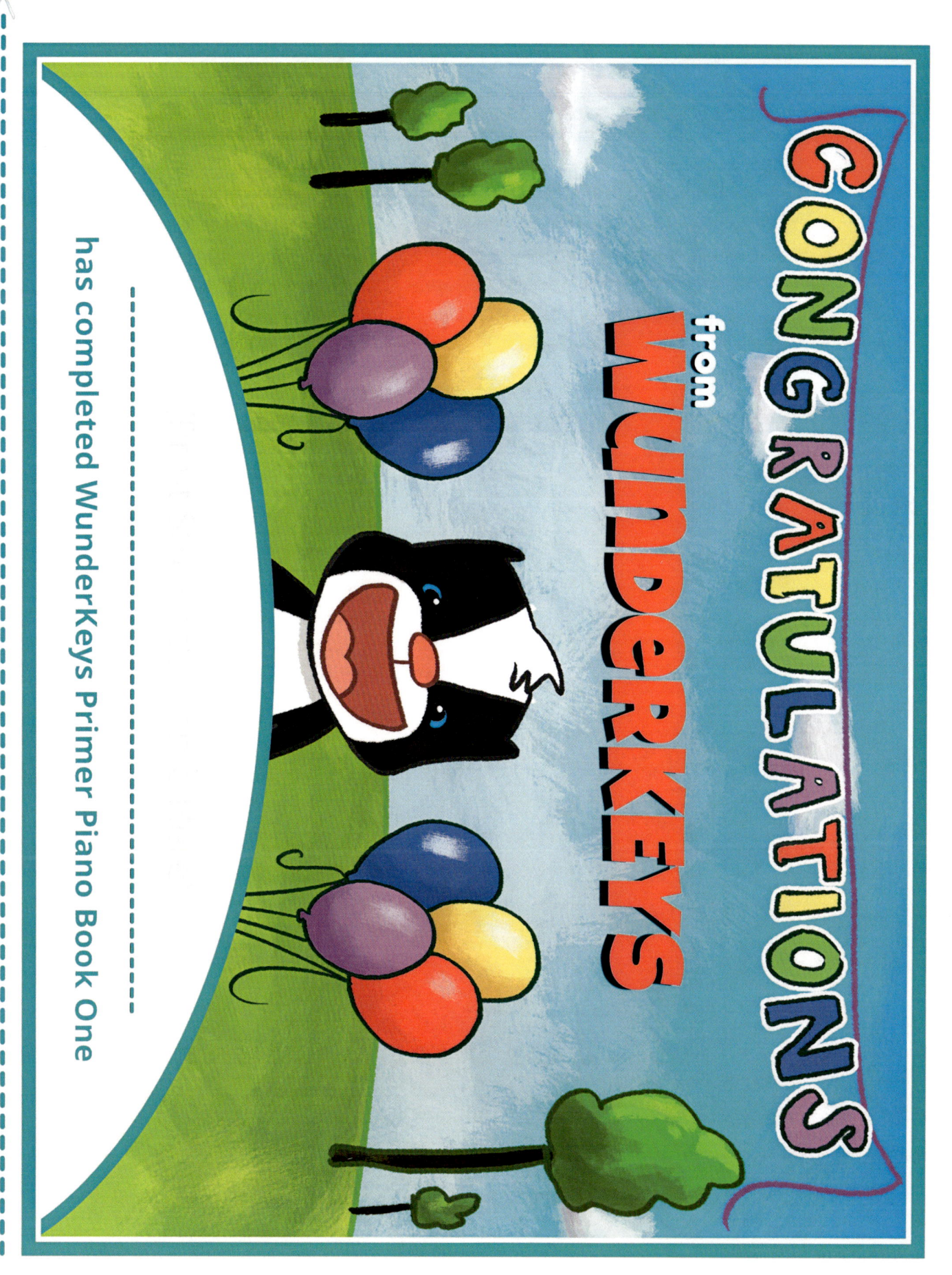

Congratulations from WunderKeys

_____ has completed WunderKeys Primer Piano Book One

Made in United States
North Haven, CT
29 August 2023